THE GOLDEN BOOK OF ROYALTY

OF ROYALTY

Relatively speaking

Robert Golden

With grateful thanks to

FLORA

The Lady Saltoun

and

DIANA

Miss FitzGeorge-Balfour

Published by

ROSVALL
ROYAL BOOKS

Enasen – Falekvarna
521 91 FALKÖPING, Sweden
tel: 46-515-37105 fax: 46-515-37165
e-mail: ted.rosvall@telia.com

ISBN 91-973978-5-7
Elanders Gummessons, Falköping 2002

FRONT COVER
Her Highness Princess Helena Victoria, 1870–1948. This granddaughter of Queen Victoria never married and was a favourite of her cousin, King George V. She is pictured in 1935 at the time of his Silver Jubilee. Her Orders are from the top: the Order of Saint John of Jerusalem, the Order of Victoria and Albert, the Order of the Crown of India and the Star and Sash of the Order of the British Empire, which she was given in 1918.

BACK COVER
The Connaught family in 'full fig' at the Coronation of George V, 1911. The Duke of Connaught (the favourite son of Queen Victoria) is seated with his Duchess, formerly Princess Louise Margaret of Prussia. At the rear, from the left: Princess Patricia of Connaught, Prince Arthur of Connaught, Crown Princess Margaret of Sweden, nee Connaught, and her husband, Crown Prince Gustav Adolf, who succeeded as King in 1950. He is wearing the robes of the Order of the Bath and his wife the robes of a Princess of Great Britain. The remainder are holding coronets which indicate their rank as a son, daughter-in-law or grandchild in the male line of a sovereign.

CONTENTS

ACKNOWLEDGMENTS

I wish to thank H.M. The Queen for gracious permission to use material from the Royal Photographic Archives and the following for their assistance in providing material and support in many ways: The late Lady May Abel Smith, Mr. Arthur Addington, Argyll Etkin Limited, H.G.D.H. Princess Margarita of Baden, the late Mary, Duchess of Beaufort, Mr. Harold Brown, the late Marchioness of Cambridge, Mr. Eric Carrera Lowe, Sir James Cayzer Bt., the Lady Mary Clayton, Miss Frances Dimond of the Royal Photographic Archives, Windsor, Martin Durrant of the V&A Photographic Archives, Mr. James Fisher, Miss Diana FitzGeorge-Balfour, Mrs. Anne Grainger, Mr. Mark Grassham, Mr. Jim Hanson, H.H. Prince Karl of Hesse, Mr. and Mrs. Miles Huntington-Whiteley, Mr and Mrs. Malcolm Liddell-Grainger, Mr. Joe Little, Janet, Marchioness of Milford Haven, the late Lady Tatiana Mountbatten, Mr. Peter Murray, Mr. Robin Piguet, the Hon. Mrs. Margaret Rhodes, Mr. Peter Russell, the Lady Saltoun, Mrs. Jane Scrivener, Mr. Ian Shapiro, Mrs Marjorie Smeeth, Mr. David Stanley, Mr. Gordon Turnbull, Mr. Hugo Vickers, the late Lady Mary Whitley, Mr. David Williamson. Especial thanks to Robert Horley for completing much of the original typescript and the entire index, an extremely tedious task, Liam Kennedy for his expert proof-reading, Trevor Wilson, my own personal travel agent who through the internet has arranged flights to Sweden and the occasional night in Gothenburg. I owe a deep debt of gratitude to my sister, Linda, who completed the original typescript only to have to re-type over 18,000 words when the computer crashed, and to Miss Charlotte Zeepvat, for so generously and promtly providing several photos for this book. I should also like to thank my publisher Ted Rosvall and his wife Margareta for being such generous hosts during my stays in Sweden. If I have inadvertently omitted to thank anyone who has given me help, I give my sincere apologies.

August 2002

Robert Golden,
5 Stockwell Avenue,
London, SW9 9SY, England

PREFACE

Since 1827, the Court Circular – the formal list recording the official engagements carried out by members of the Royal Family – has been published in The Times.

It also appears in the Daily Telegraph and is allocated as much space as is necessary. During the reign of Queen Victoria it also recorded snippets of her private life, faithfully documenting the visits of her many descendants, both British and foreign. The Queen often drafted the wording herself in order to give prominence to events which she felt should enjoy a wide circulation. She would also use its columns to promote her own views, and phrases such as 'much pleasure' or 'great regret' frequently describe her reaction to events of the day.

Up until the death of King George V in 1936 the private comings and goings of the monarch's family were given equal importance alongside the official, often mundane, duties. It was with great regularity that one could read during the 1920s and '30s entries such as 'Princess Victoria, the Duke of Connaught, Lady Patricia Ramsay, Princess Helena Victoria, Princess Marie Louise and the Dowager Marchioness of Milford Haven and the Marquess and Marchioness of Cambridge visited Their Majesties today and remained to luncheon [or tea]'. The recording of these family gatherings give one an insight into the closeness of the monarch and the extended family, providing invaluable material for historians and social chroniclers.

This mine of information covering the private family meetings ceased to be published early in the reign of King George VI. It was a gradual reduction and by 1939 it had almost disappeared; at the end of the war it was discontinued. Those engaged in researching the get-togethers of the wider Royal Family during the second half of the 20th century encounter a paucity of information; weddings and funerals are sometimes not recorded or, if mentioned, only the barest of details are listed.

Queen Mary, who lived until 1953, continued the tradition of recording visits from her family in her own Court Circular, which was issued from Marlborough House. In an entry for February 1952, at the time of the death of her son King George VI, we read that 'Her Majesty received the Margrave of Baden, Prince Ludwig of Hesse and Prince Ernst-August of Hanover'. Ernst-August had hot-footed it to Marlborough House to inform the old Queen that at a dinner held at Broadlands the previous evening Lord Mountbatten had proposed a toast to 'the House of Mountbatten', which he 'erroneously' thought was now the official name of the Royal House. Queen Mary was horrified, immediately sending for the Prime Minister, Winston Churchill, who moved quickly to ensure that the House of Windsor would continue to be the name of the monarch's family.

Many of the people who appear in the pages of this book have featured from time to time in the Court Circular. One would probably not be able to make such a claim when recording later periods of royal life.

August 2002   Robert Golden

Robert Golden published his first book 'Relatively Royal' in 2000. In this latest book, he has extended the range of those portrayed to include foreign royal relations and the FitzGeorge descendants of the 2nd Duke of Cambridge. Recently, he was involved with the Outside Broadcast Unit of BBC Television covering the Lying-in-State and Funeral of Queen Elizabeth the Queen Mother and also the Queen's Golden Jubilee Celebrations.

Six grandchildren and a great grandson of Queen Victoria at Osborne House, c.1892. Left to right: Princesses Margaret and Patricia of Connaught, Prince Waldemar of Prussia (great grandson) in the carriage, Prince Arthur of Connaught, Prince Leopold, Princess Victoria Eugenie and Prince Alexander of Battenberg (on the pony). They saw much of each other as children but lead widely divergent lives. Margaret became Crown Princess of Sweden, Victoria Eugenie married King Alfonso XIII of Spain, whilst Waldemar lived in Germany, was a haemophiliac and died in 1945 while escaping the Russian army being unable to get a necessary blood transfusion. Arthur lead an active life filled with royal duties and obligations, whilst his sister Patricia, following her marriage, merged into society and near obscurity. Leopold also suffered from haemophilia, dying in 1922 following an operation at Kensington Palace. Alexander (Drino) had a fairly uneventful life, attending major royal events and becoming a director of several companies.

Osborne, 1898. A group showing many of Queen Victoria's descendants who feature in these pages. Left to right: Prince Leopold of Battenberg (later Lord Leopold Mountbatten, grandson), Princess Aribert of Anhalt (Princess Marie Louise, granddaughter), Prince Edward of York (later Edward VIII and then Duke of Windsor, great grandson), the Duchess of York (later Queen Mary) with Princess Mary (later Princess Royal, great granddaughter), Princess Margaret of Connaught (later Crown Princess of Sweden, granddaughter), Prince Alexander of Battenberg – on ground – (later Marquess of Carisbrooke, grandson), the Duke of York (later King George V, grandson) with his son, Prince Albert of York (later King George VI), Queen Victoria, Prince Arthur of Connaught (grandson, stands behind his mother, the Duchess of Connaught), Princess Patricia of Connaught (later Lady Patricia Ramsay, granddaughter, in foreground), Princess Henry of Battenberg (Princess Beatrice, daughter), Princess Victoria Eugenie (Ena) of Battenberg (later Queen of Spain, granddaughter), Princess Helena Victoria of Schleswig-Holstein (granddaughter) and Prince Maurice of Battenberg (grandson).

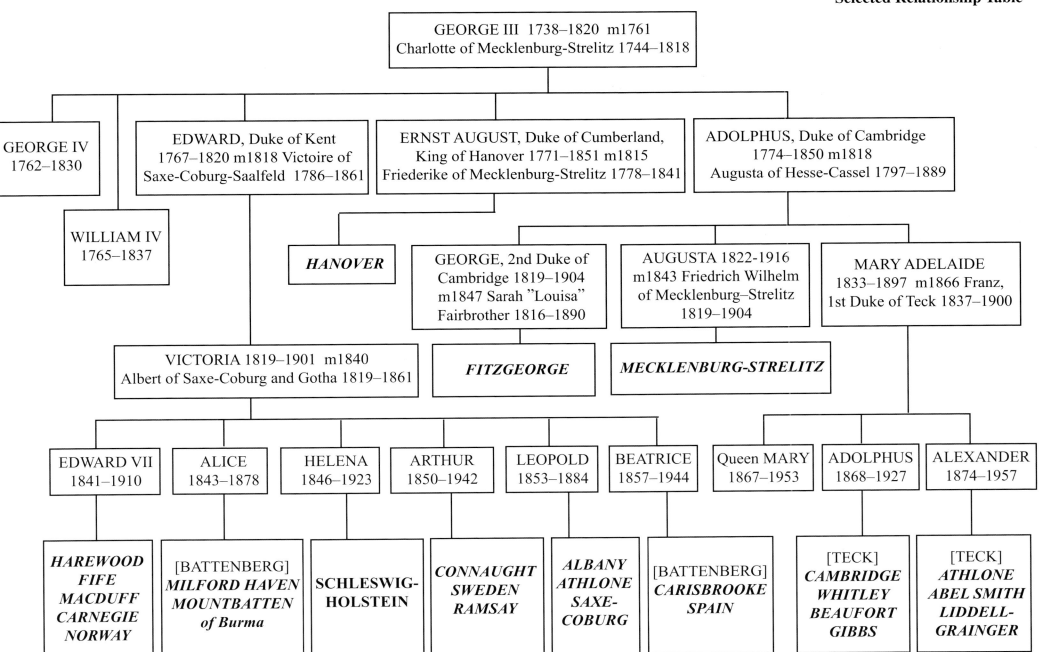

GEORGE III 1738–1820 m1761
Charlotte of Mecklenburg-Strelitz 1744–1818

GEORGE IV
1762–1830

EDWARD, Duke of Kent
1767–1820 m1818 Victoire of
Saxe-Coburg-Saalfeld 1786–1861

ERNST AUGUST, Duke of Cumberland,
King of Hanover 1771–1851 m1815
Friederike of Mecklenburg-Strelitz 1778–1841

ADOLPHUS, Duke of Cambridge
1774–1850 m1818
Augusta of Hesse-Cassel 1797–1889

WILLIAM IV
1765–1837

HANOVER

GEORGE, 2nd Duke of
Cambridge 1819–1904
m1847 Sarah "Louisa"
Fairbrother 1816–1890

AUGUSTA 1822-1916
m1843 Friedrich Wilhelm
of Mecklenburg–Strelitz
1819–1904

MARY ADELAIDE
1833–1897 m1866 Franz,
1st Duke of Teck 1837–1900

VICTORIA 1819–1901 m1840
Albert of Saxe-Coburg and Gotha 1819–1861

FITZGEORGE

MECKLENBURG-STRELITZ

EDWARD VII
1841–1910

ALICE
1843–1878

HELENA
1846–1923

ARTHUR
1850–1942

LEOPOLD
1853–1884

BEATRICE
1857–1944

Queen MARY
1867–1953

ADOLPHUS
1868–1927

ALEXANDER
1874–1957

***HAREWOOD
FIFE
MACDUFF
CARNEGIE
NORWAY***

[BATTENBERG]
***MILFORD HAVEN
MOUNTBATTEN***
of Burma

**SCHLESWIG-
HOLSTEIN**

***CONNAUGHT
SWEDEN
RAMSAY***

***ALBANY
ATHLONE
SAXE-
COBURG***

[BATTENBERG]
***CARISBROOKE
SPAIN***

[TECK]
***CAMBRIDGE
WHITLEY
BEAUFORT
GIBBS***

[TECK]
***ATHLONE
ABEL SMITH
LIDDELL-
GRAINGER***

Princess Patricia of Connaught taken at Bombay, India, during the time her father was Commander in Chief there. She looks rather uncomfortable, probably due to the heat and humidity. It was the travels with her father to exotic locations which influenced her love of the sea and lush vegetation and which are evident in her paintings. Queen Victoria allowed her to stay in India as she believed that Patricia was too young to contract diseases that might have affected her older siblings.

The Connaught girls dressed in French peasant hats from Bourbon. Patricia stands holding a model boat, Margaret seated by her side. Their mother dressed them identically until well into their teenage years. The Duchess had a frugal nature, making Patricia wear the shoes of her older sister. Unfortunately, this caused permanent damage to her feet, which became worse with the onset of old age.

Princesses Margaret and Patricia of Connaught at Balmoral, 1900. They are in mourning for their uncle, Prince Alfred, Duke of Edinburgh and Saxe-Coburg and Gotha. They did not have an altogether happy childhood – their mother, who herself had been brought up by a cold aloof mother, passed on a not dissimilar regime to her children, who in turn felt unloved and, as a result, they developed a strong and loving relationship. It was a dreadful trauma for Patricia when her sister died unexpectedly in 1920, aged 38.

Alexander Ramsay, the only child of Lady Patricia and Commander the Hon. Alexander Ramsay, was born in 1919 in the bathroom of Clarence House, the home of his grandfather the Duke of Connaught. As a child he was a playmate of the Queen and also the present Earl of Harewood. Fiercely proud of his Scotch ancestry, he lived most of his adult life north of the border, dying on the eve of his 81st birthday, 20th December 2000, at Braemar.

Charles Edward, Duke of Albany, taken at Eton, 1899. A year later he was forced to give up his English lifestyle for the more austere regime of a Potsdam Military Academy. Although only third in line to the Dukedom of Saxe-Coburg, his Connaught uncle and cousin renounced their rights, leaving Charlie with no alternative but to leave England forever. He succeeded his uncle, Alfred, as Duke in 1900 but as he was only sixteen at the time, the State was governed by a Regent, Prince Ernst of Hohenlohe-Langenburg, a son-in-law of the previous duke.

Charles Edward married, in 1905, Princess Victoria Adelheid of Schleswig-Holstein-Sonderburg-Glucksburg, a niece of the German Empress. A rather plain girl, she was a devoted mother who enjoyed the simple pleasures of family life. She was happiest of all at Callenberg, a castle set on a hill in a wooded park outside Coburg. This photograph shows her in the courtyard of the Ehrenburg Palace, Coburg, in 1913 with her four eldest children. From the left: Prince Johann Leopold, Princess Caroline Mathilde, Prince Hubertus and Princess Sibylla

At the time these photographs were taken, the Coburg children were Princes and Princesses of Great Britain with the territorial designation of Albany, and, as great grandchildren in the male line of the sovereign, held the style of 'Highness'. They lost these British styles and titles in 1917 and in 1919 the Dukedom of Albany was suspended under the Titles Deprivation Act as a direct consequence of his enemy status during the First World War. The photograph show Johann Leopold, Sibylla and Hubertus about to ski. Prince Hubertus and Princess Sibylla look on as their father prepares to ski. Both photographs were taken in 1913, in Austria.

11

Three of the four beautiful daughters of Prince Alfred, Duke of Edinburgh, and his Russian-born wife, Grand Duchess Marie. They had a peripatetic childhood following their father in his naval postings. For a time he was Commander of the Mediterranean Fleet, based in Malta, where they lived at the San Antonio Palace, outside Valetta. Marie (left) a flamboyant, theatrical woman, married King Ferdinand of Roumania, where she became an energetic nurse during World War 1. She designed in flowing Art Nouveau style the robes and regalia for her husband's Coronation in 1922. She was also a delegate to the 1919 Peace Conference at Versailles. Victoria Melita (centre), had perhaps the most tragic life of the sisters. Born in Malta, hence her second name, she was persuaded to marry her cousin, Grand Duke Ernest of Hesse, by whom she had a daughter, Elizabeth, and a stillborn son. She was later to claim that Ernest was more interested in the grooms and footmen than he was in her. The marriage ended in divorce in 1901. Her daughter Elizabeth died tragically of typhoid at 8 years old. It is said that even to this day her ghost is seen in the miniature house she played in as a child at Wolfsgarten. Her second marriage in 1905, was to another first cousin, this time on her mother's side, Grand Duke Kirill of Russia. They were not at first allowed to live in Russia, mainly due to pressure from the Tsarina, who was a sister of her first husband, and was vehemently opposed to the union. The Tsar eventually relented and they were allowed to return only to have to leave hurriedly in the wake of the Bolsheviks in 1917. They had a strenuous journey overland to Finland, finally settling at San Briac in Brittany. Alexandra (right) lead a mainly domestic life in Germany where she married the older, kindly Ernst, 7th Prince of Hohenlohe-Langenburg. They had two sons and three daughters. The two youngest daughters, Alexandra and Irma, known as Dolly and Baby in the family, were once described by a contemporary German prince as having 'been very noisy in the Hitler days'.

The youngest Edinburgh sister, Beatrice, was tall, dark and very striking. She lived in Coburg from 1893, the year her father became reigning duke. Her marriage to a Catholic cousin of King Alfonso of Spain – Infante Alfonso of Orleans-Bourbon – was not universally approved of. The couple settled in Spain but she fell foul of her cousin, Queen Ena, who accused her of meddling and being too close for comfort to the King. During the 1930s, they lived in England at Esher, when Alfonso worked in the motor car trade and mixed with people of all backgrounds and accents. In 1972 at a wedding in Seville when introduced to a young Lancastrian, he opened the conversation with 'Eee ba gum lad' in a most creditable Lancashire accent. The couple returned to live permanently in Southern Spain at San Lucar de Barrameda, where the Infanta died in 1966, the last of the sisters to survive.

12

The two daughters of Queen Victoria Eugenie of Spain (Princess Ena of Battenberg), Maria Christina (left) and Beatriz. Maria Christina was a very popular member of the Spanish royal family; handsome, fair, gregarious and a forceful presence, she enjoyed the good things of life. Following the restoration of the Spanish monarchy, she regularly appeared in Madrid attending many royal occasions. Beatriz, at the time of writing, is 93 and has the distinction of being the oldest survivor of the three remaining great grandchildren of Queen Victoria. During the 1920s and 1930s, she regularly accompanied her mother to London to visit her grandmother and namesake, Princess Beatrice. At 26, she married the Italian Don Alessandro Torlonia, Prince of Civitella-Cesi and has lived at the Torlonia Palace in Rome since then. Now confined to a wheelchair, she has not visited Spain for many years.

Lady Tatiana Mountbatten with her brother David, Earl of Medina, later 3rd Marquess of Milford Haven. Had Tatiana been born five months earlier she would have been a Princess of Battenberg, however, the hostility of the public to all things German in 1917 put paid to that. Although David was younger, he kept a watchful eye over his sister and was particularly kind to her following the death of their mother in 1963, finding a house in London and a suitable companion. After David's sudden death in 1970, Tatiana moved to St. Andrew's Hospital, Northampton. She died at Northampton General Hospital in 1988 following heart problems. Her ashes rest in Birdbrook Churchyard, Essex, close to Moyns Park, a house then owned by her nephew Ivar and where she had spent many happy holidays. David was cremated at Golders Green and his ashes are deposited in the Battenberg Chapel at Whippingham Church, Isle of Wight.

▶

Lady Mary Cambridge at a fancy dress ball, 1936. Her mother, the Marchioness of Cambridge, was patron of several charities, not least Doctor Barnardo's Homes for Children, for which she worked tirelessly. Each year, young Mary would be dressed in all sorts of improbable costumes accompanying her mother to yet another charity function. Her image appeared in a wide variety of periodicals, second only in popularity to the 'little princesses' Elizabeth and Margaret.

Prince Frederick of Teck at nine. Until Eton, he received a rather erratic education, though he was allowed free access to his parent's library. Passionately fond of classical music and collecting fine furniture, he was able to indulge his love of opera by being a regular attender at Covent Garden. Prior to 1939, each member of the royal family enjoyed unrestricted access to the Royal Box, where Freddie would often take his niece, Mary Cambridge, who was in awe of his encyclopaedic knowledge of the music and libretto. ▶

The wedding of Prince Adolphus of Teck with Lady Margaret Grosvenor, December 1894. By marrying her eldest son to a daughter of the fabulously wealthy Duke of Westminster, Princess Mary Adelaide, Duchess of Teck, hoped that some of these riches might come in her direction. The wily old Duke was only too aware of her laissez faire attitude to matters fiscal. He therefore ensured that although his daughter had a generous dowry, it was entailed to her descendants only, effectively preventing Mary Adelaide from getting her hands on even a farthing. In this photograph, the bridegroom wears the uniform of a Lieutenant of the 17th Lancers and the bride the veil previously worn by the Duchess of York (later Queen Mary) and Princess Mary Adelaide. The attendants, all members of the bride's family, are, back row, left to right: Lady Beatrice Butler and Lady Constance Grosvenor (nieces), middle row: Lady Mary Grosvenor (half-sister), Miss Millicent Grosvenor (niece), front row: Lady Helen Grosvenor (half-sister) and the Hon. Lilah Cavendish (stepmother's niece).

The christening of Princess Caroline Mathilde of Saxe-Coburg and Gotha and Great Britain, Callenberg, 1912: The Duchess of Albany regularly attended the christenings of her Coburg grandchildren where on this occasion she is shown standing at the centre of this group. Back row, left to right: Prince Albert of Schleswig-Holstein-Sonderburg-Glucksburg, Princess Caroline Mathilde of Schleswig-Holstein (Glucksburg), the Duchess of Albany, the Infante Alfonso of Orleans-Bourbon, Frau von Thuna (Lady-in-Waiting), Charles Edward, Duke of Saxe-Coburg (the child's father). Seated: Prince Philipp of Saxe-Coburg, Princess Albert of Schleswig-Holstein (Glucksburg), the Duchess of Saxe-Coburg with the infant Caroline Mathilde, the Infanta Beatrice of Orleans-Bourbon and Prince Ludwig of Bavaria, later King Ludvig III. Seated on ground: Prince Hubertus, Princess Sibylla and Prince Johann Leopold of Saxe-Coburg.

Lady Patricia Ramsay with the Marchioness of Carisbrooke leaving St. Margaret's Church, Westminster, after the marriage of Lady Mary Cambridge with the Marquess of Worcester (later Duke of Beaufort), June 1923. Lord Worcester and Lady Mary are pictured (right) at Frogmore Cottage, which had been given to her parents by King George V. Because of Court Mourning for Princess Helena, the wedding reception was cancelled but the wearing of mourning was relaxed for that day. In spite of the Duke of Beaufort's roving eye, the marriage lasted for over 60 years, though there were some bleak periods for the Duchess. On one occasion, she unburdened herself to her aunt, Queen Mary, whose advice was to remain married, citing the Duke's father as having been just the same, but he always returned to his wife.

Lady Patricia Ramsay at St. James's Palace following her wedding to Commander the Hon. Alexander Ramsay, 1919. Extremely good-looking, Princess Patricia received several offers of marriage before settling on her Scottish naval officer. King Alfonso of Spain and the heir to the throne of Portugal were among the suitors she rejected. Her wedding dress and train were recently given by her daughter-in-law, Lady Saltoun, to the Museum of Princess Patricia's Canadian Light Infantry at Calgary.

The newly-engaged Princess Ingrid of Sweden and Crown Prince Frederik of Denmark pose with her grandfather, the Duke of Connaught, at Bagshot Park, 1935. The Duke was devoted to his Swedish granddaughter and was a little alarmed at Frederik's (Rico) capacity for alcohol. A decade earlier Rico had briefly been engaged to Princess Olga of Greece who broke it off because of his drinking habits. Ingrid was made of sterner stuff: she soon ensured that he curtailed his excesses.

The wedding of Captain Alexander Ramsay with the Hon. Flora Fraser, 1956. The loss of a leg in the Second World War did not deter Captain Ramsay from wearing the kilt, which he did throughout his married life. His bride is simply attired. She carried neither flowers nor wore jewellery apart from a circlet of pink and white pearls in her head-dress and she did not have bridesmaids. Standing left to right: Major David Fraser (bride's cousin), Admiral the Hon. Sir Alexander Ramsay, Lieutenant Colonel Peter Thorne (best man), bridegroom and bride, the Hon. Elizabeth Ormsby-Gore (bride's best friend), Lord Saltoun (bride's father) and the Hon. Mrs. Wardlaw-Ramsay (bride's paternal aunt). Seated: Lady Patricia Ramsay, Queen Ingrid of Denmark, Queen Elizabeth the Queen Mother and Lady Saltoun (bride's mother). The wedding had taken place at St. Peter's Church, Fraserburgh, close to the bride's ancestral home, Cairnbulg Castle.

Lady Louise Mountbatten married, as his second wife, Crown Prince Gustav Adolf of Sweden in November 1923 at the Chapel Royal, St. James's Palace. Having reached the age of 34, the bride was somewhat reluctant to have a full scale white wedding. It was only when her uncle, the Grand Duke of Hesse, sent a length of shimmering silver sari material that she could be persuaded to wear traditional dress. In this photograph taken in Princess Beatrice's apartments at Kensington Palace she is surrounded by her nieces and nephew. Standing, l to r: Princesses Cecelie and Theodora of Greece and Prince Wilhelm of Sweden (best man and brother of bridegroom). Seated: Princess Sophie of Greece, bridegroom and bride and Princess Margarita of Greece. At front: Earl of Medina and Lady Tatiana Mountbatten.

A group taken at Claridge's after the wedding of David, Marquess of Milford Haven and Miss Janet Bryce, 1960. David had been married previously in 1950 to an American, another Mrs. Simpson, but had divorced her in Mexico in 1954 and again in England in 1960. Due to his divorced status, they could not marry in an Anglican church so the ceremony took place at the Presbyterian Church of St. Andrew, Frognal, London. Standing, left to right: Earl Mountbatten of Burma, Colonel Harold Phillips, bridegroom and bride, Mr. Patrick Broome (best man), Sir Harold Wernher and Mr. John Bryce (cousin to the bride). Seated: Lady Zia Wernher, Queen Louise of Sweden, the bride's mother Mrs. Francis Bryce with Michael Naylor-Leyland, Lady Tatiana Mountbatten, Mrs. John Bryce and Mrs. Harold Phillips (now Lady Kennard, daughter of Lady Zia Wernher). The bridesmaids: Maralyn Butter, Amanda Naylor-Leyland, Rohays Butter and Marita and Fiona Phillips.

21

Following the funeral of Lady May Abel Smith at St. George's Chapel, Windsor, in June 1994, a lunch was held at her home, Barton Lodge, Winkfield. Her cousin, Princess Juliana of the Netherlands had a splendid time meeting lots of relations and old friends there. She became so engrossed that she had to be hurried along to her waiting car so she would not miss a 'Purple Air Corridor' to Amsterdam. This photograph, taken by the author, shows Princess Juliana being escorted to her car by Mrs. Elizabeth Wise (left) and Mrs. Richard Abel Smith.

◀ Elizabeth Abel Smith was married in 1965 at St. Paul's Church. Knightsbridge, to Mr. Peter Wise. Her godmother, Queen Elizabeth the Queen Mother was present as was her cousin Princess Sibylla of Sweden. As the bride walked down the aisle, a brown collie dog shot passed her landing at the feet of the Queen Mother and, in the process, nearly tripping the bride up. It took some persuasion to get it out into the street again. Standing, left to right: Captain and Mrs. Anthony Wise (groom's parents), Princess Marina Duchess of Kent, bridegroom and bride, Mr. Alan Tritton (best man), Lady May Abel Smith (bride's mother), Princess Sibylla of Sweden and Colonel Sir Henry Abel Smith (bride's father). Front row: Nicholas Hill, Georgina Baillie, Olivia Coleman, Katherine Abel Smith (facing bride), Louise Huntington-Whiteley (in front), Charles Liddell-Grainger, Queen Elizabeth the Queen Mother, Fiona Baillie and Ian Liddell-Grainger.

The christening of Katherine Abel Smith, St. Peter's Church, Cranbourne, 1961. Through Queen Emma of the Netherlands and her sister the Duchess of Albany, the Dutch royal family are closely related to the Abel Smith branch of our royal family. The ties were strengthened in 1940 when Princess Juliana and her children went to live in Canada near to Princess Alice and Lord Athlone, when he was Governor General. At the same time, Anne, Richard and Elizabeth Abel Smith were there for the duration of the war; the two families seeing one another regularly. Left to right: Mr. Tim Kendrew, Mrs. Richard Abel Smith (formerly Marcia Kendrew), Crown Princess Beatrix of the Netherlands holding Katherine, Captain Richard Abel Smith, Princess Alice Countess of Athlone, Nurse Pooley and Sir Nicholas Nuttall who had been best man at the wedding of Richard and Marcia in 1960.

The Golden Wedding of the Earl and Countess of Strathmore (parents of Queen Elizabeth the Queen Mother – then Duchess of York), Glamis Castle, 1931. On her father's side, the present Queen has had seven first cousins but her mother's family provided a vast tribe of 23, of which six survive. Queen Elizabeth the Queen Mother outlived 17 of her nephews and nieces as well as a daughter. Some of these Strathmore first cousins are portrayed in this group. The brackets following their names refer to their relationship to the present Queen. Back row, l to r: Hon. Elizabeth Elphinstone (cousin), Hon. Jean Elphinstone (cousin), Hon. Cecilia Bowes Lyon (cousin), Hon. John Bowes Lyon (cousin), the Duke of York, Henry Streatfield (who had been best man at the wedding in 1881), Hon. Michael Bowes Lyon (uncle), Gavin Ralston (factor at Glamis Castle), Hon. David Bowes Lyon (uncle), Lord Elphinstone (uncle), the Master of Elphinstone (cousin) and Hon. Mrs. Michael Bowes Lyon (aunt). Middle row: Hon. Mrs. David Bowes Lyon with Davinia (aunt and cousin), Countess Granville (aunt), Lady Elphinstone (aunt), the Duchess of York with Princess Margaret of York, the Earl and Countess of Strathmore, Lord and Lady Glamis (uncle and aunt) and Lady Christian Martin (aunt). Front row: (all those in the front row are cousins), Lady Mary Leveson Gower, Hon. Andrew Elphinstone, Hon. Margaret Elphinstone, Diana Cinderella Bowes Lyon, Fergus Bowes Lyon, Princess Elizabeth of York, Anne Bowes Lyon, Hon. Timothy Bowes Lyon, Hon. Nancy Bowes Lyon, Lord Leveson and Rosemary Bowes Lyon. Diana Cinderella, a daughter of the Hon. John Bowes Lyon, was a bridesmaid to the Queen along with the Hon. Margaret Elphinstone. Once, while declaring a tea room open at Fettercairn, Diana quipped: 'this is one Cinderella who won't be washing the dishes'.

24

A Danish prince marries into the Bowes Lyon family, Glamis Castle, 1950. His Highness Prince Georg of Denmark (a second cousin of King George VI) married Anne, the former wife of Viscount Anson and daughter of the Hon. John Bowes Lyon, a brother of the then Queen. At that time, Denmark had strict rules regarding marriages of members of the royal family. Normally, Prince Georg, upon marrying a commoner would have lost his royal style and title becoming a Count of Rosenborg as had his younger brother, Prince Flemming, upon marrying a Danish commoner the previous year. As the bride was a niece of the Queen of England, it would have been considered insulting to the British royal house if she were not allowed to take her husband's rank, and so he remained a Danish prince. Because of the rigid attitudes to divorce which then prevailed, it was thought inappropriate for the Queen and Princess Margaret to attend the service, but they were able to be present at the reception. Standing, l to r: Countess Granville, the Earl of Strathmore, Princess Josephine Charlotte of Luxembourg, Prince Carl Bernadotte, Princess Ragnhild of Norway, Crown Prince of Olav of Norway, Earl Granville, bride and bridegroom, Count Flemming of Rosenborg, Princess Astrid of Norway, Mr. Simon Bowes Lyon, Miss Diana Cinderella Bowes Lyon, Princess Margaret, the Hon. David Bowes Lyon and Countess Ruth of Rosenborg. Seated: Lady Clinton and Lord Clinton (bride's maternal grandparents), the Queen, Princess Margaretha of Denmark and Prince Axel of Denmark (groom's parents) and the Hon. Mrs. Fenella Bowes Lyon (bride's mother). Sitting in front are the bride's children: the Hon. Patrick Anson (now Earl of Lichfield) and the Hon. Elizabeth Anson (now Lady Elizabeth Shakerley).

It is hard to think of a single member of the royal family who has not at some time appeared on the balcony of Buckingham Palace. Most of the appearances are at the annual Sovereign's Birthday Parade, when members of the royal family bring their children and grandchildren (who are not always royal) to watch the flypast. This line up was taken in 1937 and shows, from the left, unidentified lady, Lady May Abel Smith, Princess Elizabeth, the Princess Royal, Princess Margaret, the Queen, Princess Marie Louise, the Master of Carnegie, Princess Helena Victoria, Queen Mary, the Duchess of Kent, the Duchess of Gloucester, Lady Maud and Captain Lord Carnegie, Major Henry Abel Smith and Lord Frederick Cambridge.

The royal family are wearing Half-Mourning for King George VI in this photograph of 1952. From the left: Queen Elizabeth the Queen Mother, the Queen, the Duke of Gloucester, the Marchioness of Carisbrooke, the Princess Royal, the Duke of Edinburgh, Prince Richard of Gloucester, Princess Margaret, Lady Patricia Ramsay, Princess Alice Countess of Athlone, the Marquis of Cambridge, unidentified lady, the Duke of Beaufort partly hidden, the Marchioness of Cambridge, Lady May Abel Smith and Lady Mary Whitley.

Bagshot Park, 1893. A house party for Ascot shows a rare glimpse of the Duke and Duchess of Connaught as hosts to the Duke and Duchess of Edinburgh. The Duchess of Edinburgh was not fond of the English social scene and was very relieved when, in 1893, her husband succeeded as Duke of Saxe-Coburg and Gotha thus giving her status as the leading lady, with precedence immediately after her husband and not below her husband's sisters, which had been the case in this country. Front row: the Duke of Connaught, the Duchess of Edinburgh, the Duke of Edinburgh and the Duchess of Connaught. The remainder are not royal and only the gentleman standing at the back wearing a bow tie has been identified. He is Maurice Bourke, a leading socialite of the time.

Four branches of the royal family are photographed at Balmoral in 1900, all in the deepest mourning for the Duke of Saxe-Coburg and Gotha and Edinburgh. Prince Heinrich of Prussia, a grandson of Queen Victoria through his mother the Princess Royal, Empress Frederick, sports the Balmoral tartan. Princess Patricia of Connaught, at 14, is not yet old enough to wear a full length skirt. Princess Heinrich of Prussia, born Princess Irene of Hesse, was another grandchild of Queen Victoria. Her mother was Princess Alice, the third child of the Queen. Irene married her first cousin Heinrich and lived a long and full life in Germany. She had the sorrow of knowing that she had two sons who suffered from haemophilia. Princess Margaret of Connaught and the Duchess of York (later Queen Mary) complete the group.

Charlie, Duke of Saxe-Coburg and Gotha and Albany, with his family, Callenberg, 1908. The Duke stands in the centre with his father-in-law, Friedrich Ferdinand, Duke of Schleswig-Holstein of the Glucksburg branch of that family, on his right, and his brother-in-law Friedrich on his left. This Friedrich married yet another descendant of Queen Victoria, Princess Marie Melita of Hohenlohe-Langenburg, a granddaughter of her second son, Alfred, Duke of Edinburgh and Saxe-Coburg and Gotha, whom Charlie had succeeded as reigning duke in 1900. Seated, next to the empty pram, is 'Dick', Duchess of Saxe-Coburg and Gotha and Albany. The Duchess of Albany is holding her grandson, Prince Johann Leopold. Perched just behind in a precarious fashion is Princess Sibylla and then Caroline Mathilde, Duchess of Schleswig-Holstein who was born a princess of the Augustenburg branch of the Schleswig-Holstein tribe. The image of Princess Sibylla has been cut from another photograph and pasted on. Perhaps she was misbehaving when the group was taken and had to be photographed later?

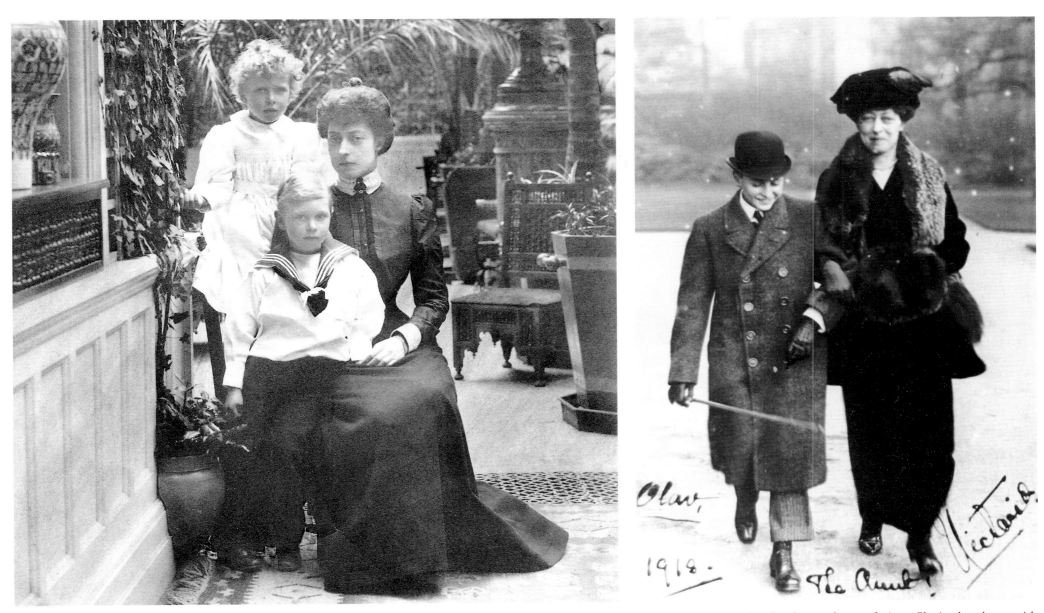

Olav,
1918.
The Aunt
Victoria

Princess Victoria, the unmarried daughter of King Edward VII and Queen Alexandra, with Prince Edward of Wales and Princess Mary of Wales, her nephew and niece. She is also shown with another nephew, Crown Prince Olav of Norway. Although the Princess was fond of her nephews and nieces, her affection was not always reciprocated. A thwarted romance and the constant demands made by her mother had caused her to develop into a waspish, disillusioned woman. Following her mother's death in 1925, she enjoyed her new found freedom by buying a house, Coppins, at Iver in Buckinghamshire, where she became popular in the village. A favourite trick was to turn up unannounced at the village school where she often disrupted the classes. She would also appear at the classroom window, pull faces at the children, who fell into gales of laughter, and disappear before the teacher could spot the cause of the merriment.

31

Princess Maud, the youngest daughter of Edward VII and Queen Alexandra, married her first cousin, Prince Charles of Denmark, who was elected King of Norway in 1905 at the time it became independent from Sweden. Taking the name Haakon, he and his wife are seen here with their son, Crown Prince Olav, who himself became Norway's second monarch of modern times. Haakon was a brilliant monarch who reigned for over 52 years. When in 1928 a Government crisis catapulted the Marxist Social Democrats into power, the King in spite of strong opposition supported the change. When after a mere 14 days that Government collapsed, the King remarked, 'you have to remember that I am the King of the Communists too'. In exile in London during the Second World War, he made frequent broadcasts to his people from Bush House. On one occasion, when arriving at the studio, he was asked by a rather confused receptionist, 'sorry, dear, where did you say you were king of?'

Buckingham Palace, 1937. Queen Maud of Norway (centre) with Crown Prince Olav and Crown Princess Martha. Until 1937, there was no precedent for either a Queen Dowager or a foreign crowned head to be present at the Coronation ceremony. Queen Mary changed that when she attended her son's Coronation and this made it possible for his Aunt Maud to be there. Queen Maud is wearing her robes as a Princess of Great Britian; she also wears the base of the crown which had belonged to her mother Queen Alexandra.

The 70th Birthday of Princess Sophie of Hanover, June 1984. The favourite sister of Prince Philip and a much loved aunt of the Prince of Wales is photographed with her extended family at Schloss Friedrichsof, Kronberg, Germany. The house was built by the widowed eldest child of Queen Victoria – Victoria the German Empress – and named in honour of her husband the Emperor Frederick. Sophie's first husband Prince Christopher of Hesse had been brought up in the house which is now a luxury hotel, containing many of the Empress's possessions. Front row, l to r: The Duke of Edinburgh, Princess Margaret of Hesse, Prince Georg Wilhelm of Hanover, Princess Vera of Hanover with her grandmother Princess Sophie, the Prince and Princess of Wales, Princess Irina of Hesse, Princess and Prince Karl of Hesse. Second row, l to r: Prince and Princess Welf of Hanover, Princess Marianne of Baden, Princess Charlotte and Prince Kraft of Hohenlohe-Langenburg, Prince Georg of Hanover with Princess Nora of Hanover, Prince and Princess Wolfgang of Hesse and Prince Ludwig of Baden. Third row, from extreme left: Princess Elizabeth of Hesse and Count Friedrich von Oppersdorff, Princess Frederika of Hanover with her husband Jerry Cyr, Prince Christopher of Yugoslavia and his then fiancé, Clarissa von Lerchenfeld, unidentified lady, Princess Beatrix of Hohenlohe-Langenburg, Princess and Prince Ernst August of Hanover and the Landgrave of Hesse. Fourth row, l to r: Princess Margarita of Baden, Princess Christina, Mrs. Van Eyck, Princess Clarissa of Windisch-Graetz, Princess Marina of Windisch-Graetz, Princess Georg of Hanover, the Margravine and Margrave of Baden and Prince Rainer of Hesse.

Prince Arthur of Connaught was Governor General of the Union of South Africa from 1920–23. Upon returning to England, he and Princess Arthur launched into a frenzy of visiting family and friends, taking up again the routine they had abandoned four years previously. In the left photograph, taken at Bagshot Park during Ascot week, Prince Arthur stands with his sister, Lady Patricia Ramsay, whose son, Sandy, stands in front. Princess Arthur is sitting next to the Duke of Connaught. The 'Arthurs' link arms with their son, the Earl of Macduff, at Mar Lodge, Braemar, Aberdeenshire. Nursing apart, Princess Arthur was never happier than when living an outdoor life in the bracing climate of this Scottish estate, which she had inherited from her father in 1912. Until the War and permanent ill-health made it impossible, she came here every summer and autumn until 1940. Early in the war, she took in evacuees from Glasgow, who were not in the least grateful for her efforts in making them welcome. They argued amongst themselves, and the children were peevish and afraid of the remoteness of the place. It did not last long. The women being alarmed at the thought of what their husbands might be up to with the neighbours, soon beat a hasty retreat – much to the relief of Princess Arthur.

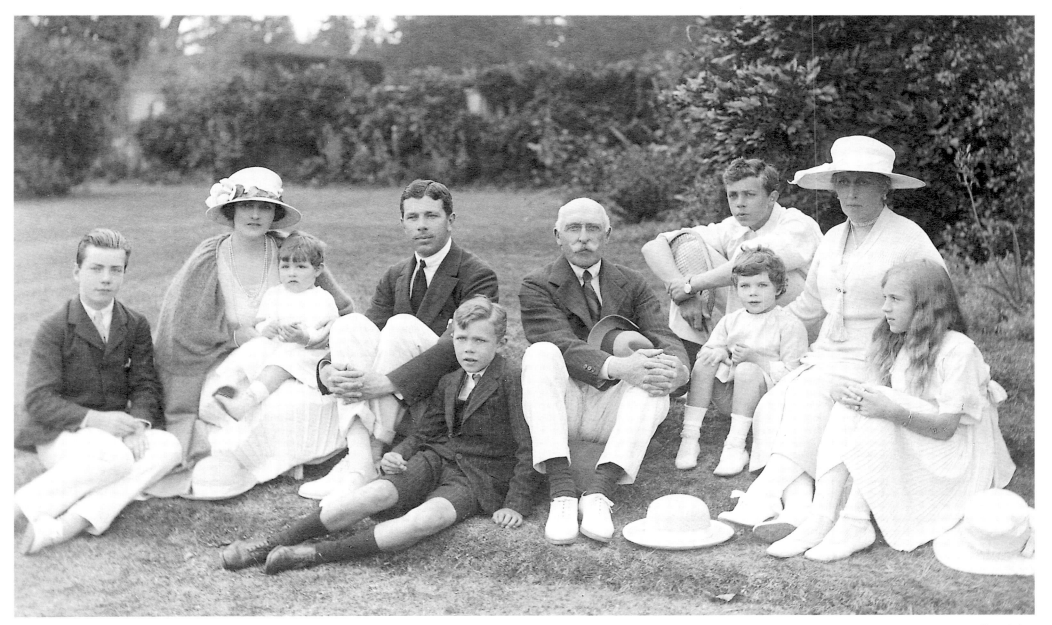

The widowed son-in-law of the Duke of Connaught, Crown Prince Gustav Adolf of Sweden, with his children, on a visit to Bagshot Park, 1921. Princess Helena Victoria got on well with her Connaught relations who felt that she might fill the void in the life of the Crown Prince and his family. Nothing came of these hopes, although she remained on good terms with her Swedish cousins, seeing them regularly. Left to right: Prince Sigvard, Lady Patricia Ramsay with Sandy, Crown Prince Gustav Adolf, Prince Bertil, the Duke of Connaught, Prince Gustav Adolf (Edmund), Prince Carl Johan (Johnny – one of the three remaining great grandchildren of Queen Victoria) in front, Princess Helena Victoria and Princess Ingrid.

For a Victorian, the Duchess of Connaught was quite liberated having written a number of intimate letters to her fiance which he destroyed as he told her they were so private that he did not want them to be seen by anyone else's eyes. She even confided to him that her grandfather, Prince Karl of Prussia, wanted to know 'how far they went', and that the very same (Prince Karl) had once even tried to take advantage of her before a hunting expedition. When her first child, Princess Margaret, was born in 1882, she breastfed her; a practice virtually unknown at that time in royal and aristocratic circles.

The Duke of Connaught at Tel-el-Kebir, 1882. The battle of Tel-el-Kebir in Egypt was a very active theatre of war and is where Prince Arthur commanded the Guards Brigade Egyptian Expeditionary Force. He came under sustained bombardment from shell fire and was reported to have 'sat on his horse on a bit of rising ground as coolly as possible and was not seen to attempt to move or duck his head, although some shells passed precious close to him'. On his return to London after a successful campaign, he was greeted by wildly enthusiastic crowds.

A young Duchess of Connaught, dressed up as her great-grandmother, the famous Queen Luise of Prussia (1776–1810). Luise, who was a duchess of Mecklenburg-Strelitz and an aunt by marriage of Princess Augusta of Cambridge, is the third generation of a unique series of nine Luises of direct descent, starting with Luise of Hesse-Darmstadt, née Leiningen (1729–1818) and ending with Princess Luise of Prussia (b 1917).

This photograph of Princess Patricia of Connaught taken about 1907, was one of a series made into picture postcards which sold by the thousand. At this time, she had started to carry out royal engagements, often with her parents and occasionally on her own. She accompanied her father and mother to South Africa in 1910 when he inaugurated the first Union Parliament where she sat on the left of the throne. She occupied a similar place when her father performed the same duty in Canada. On safari in Kenya in 1909, she suddenly became ill, her temperature soaring, however, castor oil and some native medicine soon had her on her feet again.

Princess Patricia sits in the studio of Clare Sheriden behind a plaster model of a sculpture of herself, 1918. It is thought that only the head and shoulders were completed. She was an enthusiastic supporter of artists, often attending private viewings of young, largely unknown painters and sculptors. A prodigious painter in oils and watercolours, she held four exhibitions devoted to her own work. In her memoirs of 1956 her cousin, Princess Marie Louise, rather disparagingly describes her works as 'modern – in fact, very modern' though conceding that she was not sufficiently 'up' in the expression of modern art to appreciate all her pictures. As well as pupils of Gauguin, she also counted Barbara Hepworth among her friends and mentors.

Prince Arthur of Connaught as a 'Wet Bob' at Eton, c.1899. At Eton College if you row you are described as a wet bob. Those who play rugger are dry bobs.

The oldest Grenadier and the youngest Ensign – the Duke of Connaught with his grandson Alexander Ramsay. A close bond between the two had been forged when the Duke often looked after Sandy when, as a boy, his father was posted abroad on naval duties. During the school holidays, Sandy would liven up the quiet, sober atmosphere of Clarence House and Bagshot Park. It was a source of great pride and satisfaction to the duke when his grandson chose the Grenadiers as his regiment and not follow his own father into the Navy. Thirty-three years separate the Duke being appointed Colonel of the Grenadier Guards and his grandson joining them. The Duke found Sandy's approach to his soldiering much more sound than that of his other English grandson, Alastair, Earl of Macduff, who was vague and seemed incapable of applying his mind to the task in hand.

The Duke of Connaught as Colonel, Grenadier Guards, 1929. Always erect and handsome, none more so that when in uniform, he was attracted to and by good-looking young women. An early attraction had been Princess Mary, the younger daughter of King George V of Hanover, and therefore his second cousin. He courted her at a distance in the 1870s and, in spite of several meetings, they were rarely left alone. Although his feelings for her grew in intensity, hers did not really develop. She eventually announced that whilst she was fond of him she could never really love him. Privately, she was in love with an older man who was unavailable and she died unmarried in 1904, aged 54. In later years, whilst on a diplomatic mission to Greece, the Duke was very taken by the young Aspasia Manos, the Greek-born commoner who was in love with and later married King Alexander I. ►

39

The Earl of Macduff and his parents, Prince and Princess Arthur of Connaught, in 1935. Princess Arthur was affected throughout her life by the premature deaths of those closest to her. In 1912, her father, the Duke of Fife, died after being shipwrecked off North Africa and her mother, the Princess Royal, who was never strong, died aged 64 in 1931. Prince Arthur developed cancer and died at their home in Belgrave Square, aged 55 – his father went to visit him shortly before his death and was relieved to find him sleeping peacefully; he had dreaded the thought of saying a final goodbye. Ten days after Prince Arthur's death, Macduff was sent to Palestine with his regiment: his mother did not see him for over four years. He too died early, in 1943, while staying at Government House, Ottawa, at the age of 28. The final straw came in 1945, when her beloved sister, Maudie, the Countess of Southesk, died suddenly following an asthma attack leaving a son of 15, Lord Carnegie. He and a group of fellow Etonians were waiting on the platform at the railway station, having just gone down for Christmas, when a policeman approached Carnegie, ascertained his identity before taking him off to an office to break the news that his mother was dead. Princess Arthur lived until 1959 when, after years of being bedridden from arthritis, she died aged 67.

The Princes Maurice, Alexander and Leopold of Battenberg dressed for the Coronation of King George V, 1911. All three were on active service during the First World War which demonstrated particular bravery on the part of the haemophiliac Leopold. In spite of Maurice's gallantry and death at Mons and the undoubted loyalty of the brothers, the family was forced to change their name to the more English-sounding Mountbatten. It must have been distressing for their mother, Princess Beatrice, to have to discard her husband's name, especially as he had died fighting for the British in the Ashanti War having contracted typhoid in 1896 .

▶

Princess Alice of Battenberg taken about the time she married Prince Andrew of Greece, 1903. Alice was the fourth great grandchild of Queen Victoria and was born at Windsor in 1885 in the same room and the same bed in which her own mother, Victoria of Hesse, had been born. She was deaf from birth, her mother teaching her to lip-read; a skill which came in very useful in later years when she could follow conversations in a number of languages. After the exile of Prince Andrew from Greece in 1922, she and her family lived at St. Cloud, Paris, existing largely on funds provided by the extremely wealthy wife of Andrew's brother George, Princess Marie Bonaparte. For much of the 1930s, she was confined to sanatoriums, having suffered a mental breakdown. She became obsessed with a religious fervour believing she was 'the bride of Christ'. After seven years, she was sufficiently recovered to take up a semblance of family life returning to Greece where she eventually founded the Sisterhood of Martha and Mary on the Island of Tinos. On her visits to the Queen, Prince Philip and her English grandchildren, she appeared a shadowy, strange looking figure in her nun's habit. In reality, she was never trained as a nun and her attitude towards the rules of her own convent was relaxed to say the least, exceeding by months the rule that only four weeks holiday could be taken each year. In 1967, at the time of the Colonels' coup in Athens, she was invited by the Queen to live in Buckingham Palace, where she died peacefully in December 1969.

Prince George of Teck, 1919, later 2nd Marquess of Cambridge. During World War Two, George Cambridge commanded a battalion of the R.A.S.C., bringing them all home safely from Dunkirk. He wrote frequently to his wife Dorothy and in a letter of April 1940 he tells her that 'Aunt May (Queen Mary) has sent to me another cake and an enormous slab of chocolate, which is kind of her but not very good for my uniform' and 'I should try and see Aunt and Uncle (the Athlones) before they depart for Canada'. 'You can tell them that we will all come out and visit them when this ghastly mess is over, if the grateful country pays me a gratuity'. In another note, he enquires about his sister Mary's boils and hopes she can now sit on a firm chair. He also tries to visualise where her bungalow might be 'I can't think whereabouts Mary's bungalow is, as Eton Wick used to be rather a slummy sort of place'. Referring to his late brother-in-law's family, he remarks on 7th May 1940 that 'I saw Anna Gibbs was engaged to someone with a funny name, I think she is worth a handbag'. On his 17th wedding anniversary he remembered that 'the 10th of April always seems to be cold and today is no exception but it is sunny, very like the day my own dear darling when we walked down the aisle together and you made me the happiest man alive'.

The first Lady Cambridge when Duchess of Teck, about 1910. She and her husband were seldom apart throughout their married life, she even travelled with him to the Boer War. Essentially a country woman, she shied away from large court functions except when her husband's presence required her attendance at his side. She got on very well with her sister-in-law Queen Mary as they had many interests in common especially sharing a love of antiques. She freely admitted to having an intense dislike of Prussians but she had a great affection for Austrians having made many friendships during the time her husband was Military Attaché in Vienna. When Lord Cambridge died she returned to London to be near Queen Mary living at a Grosvenor Estate-owned house in Eaton Place.

Adolphus, Marquess of Cambridge, had a kindly heart but could be brusque and off-hand: he did not suffer fools gladly. He had inherited the 'Teck temper' which was ferocious to behold, suddenly exploding in the most frightening manner but just as suddenly abating when he carried on as normal. His father, the Duke of Teck, passed on this trait to him as well as to Prince Alexander (Earl of Athlone) and, through Queen Mary (though she herself was very calm), it passed down to King George VI. The Marquess, a man of stentorian tones, was overheard by his future daughter-in-law, Dorothy Hastings, while on a pre-engagement visit, discussing her with his wife, 'well, she's not much to look at but she is a lady'. Dorothy had a very ambivalent opinion of this description of herself. Along with his sister May, he was confirmed in the Private Chapel of Kensington Palace and from that day he never missed attending church on Sundays.

Lord Frederick Cambridge, the younger son of Adolphus, Marquess of Cambridge, was described by Osbert Sitwell as 'a charming and lively personality, with a little of the air of an 18th century prince'. He certainly cut quite a figure, his handsome looks attracting him to a string of women. During the 1930s, he served with the Coldstream Guards in Palestine where according to letters to his sisters, life was fairly quiet, if not downright boring at times. His time was occupied with showing parties of troops around holy places in the old city, admitting that his biblical history was on the weak side. He went bathing in the sea at Jaffa, played numerous polo matches, 'that foul game tennis' and some sand grouse shooting for good measure. Mess life was highly civilised with dining in the garden on the banks of the Blue Nile followed by high jinks in the dormitories where he ended by 'being slippered by Ronnie Dawnay, who is known as the prefect'. On 10th December 1936, he writes to his brother, 'George, what a terrible thing all this is. I heard about the Abdication on the wireless half an hour after Mr. Baldwin had given it out in the House of Commons. Indeed, I am sorry for the Queen, one wonders what will happen next'. Freddie was killed in action in Belgium in May 1940.

A triple portrait of the Marchioness of Cambridge which featured in the The Sketch, 1936. During the 1920s and 30s, Dorothy Cambridge frequently appeared in the list of 'best dressed women'. In later life, she took great delight in attending royal occasions wearing clothes she had bought at her village jumble sales; outfits she wore with supreme élan. In 1974, she produced for charity 'The Royal Blue and Gold Cook Book' which contained recipes from members of the royal family and other well-known personalities. Its production was held up for some six months due to the Queen Mother being tardy in providing a promised recipe on time. When it arrived it required the use of so many eggs as to be unsuitable for present day consumption. Lady Cambridge, who was an adventurous cook, felt that on one occasion her inventiveness might have gone too far. During the war, she was presented with a whole salmon and finding she had no olive oil with which to make the mayonnaise substituted liquid paraffin. Four people enjoyed a lunch of cold salmon mayonnaise, all having second helpings, and, as far as she knew, no one suffered any ill-effects.

Lady Mary Cambridge, taken in 1950, with her dog, Rowley. This King Charles spaniel she admitted had the sexual appetite of his namesake with the same cavalier attitude. As a girl staying at Sandringham for Christmases, she and Princess Elizabeth would be summoned to say goodnight to old King George V. They would clamber over a pile of Red Boxes, sit on his knee and, as a reward, receive a very whiskery kiss. As she matured her photographs appeared in all the society magazines often ending up as a pin-up in many a soldier and sailor's sleeping quarters. She and her mother were often given discarded dresses by Queen Mary who had no conception that the elaborate styles she wore were totally unsuitable as normal everyday apparel. By the time the complex whalebone supports were removed, the garments became quite shapeless.

Anne Abel Smith at her 'Coming Out' 1950. Very much part of the social scene both as a debut-ante and following her marriage to David Liddell-Grainger in 1957, when she became the chatelaine of a large castle in the Borders. Her life now as a missionary in Africa could not be in greater contrast to her youth.

Elizabeth Abel Smith, 1954. Born at Kensington Palace and christened at St.Mary Abbot's Church, where her nanny held her shoulder high parading her up and down the aisles in order to give the public a better view. She was one of the royal relations who accompanied the Queen and Prince Philip to Stockholm for the Equestrian Olympic Games in 1954, staying at The Royale Palace in Stockholm. She now lives in the Cotswolds where she is a vigorous walker covering many miles in a day.

Lady Iris Mountbatten looking very self-assured and sophisticated for someone of 17. A Train-Bearer for the Queen at the 1937 Coronation, she is photographed in her drawing room at Kensington Palace wearing the silver dress which she had worn at the first Court of that year. Tall and talented, she rebelled against the restrictions imposed by her grandmother, Princess Beatrice, with whom she and her parents lived. At 16, she acquired a motorcycle which she rode fast and furiously along the palace driveway, claiming later to be the first woman in England to hold a motorbike licence. Her last home was in Cabbage Town, Toronto, where she mixed with a bohemian circle of musicians, writers and poets. In 1956, she had planned to write her memoirs which were to include her life with the royal family. Fortunately, this potentially embarrassing project was dropped in favour of writing a comedy which she hoped would be produced on Broadway. Sadly, when she died in 1982, none of her royal relations attended the funeral nor did they send representatives. The British High Commission also declined an invitation to send a representative.

Nada, Marchioness of Milford Haven was the younger daughter of Grand Duke Michael Michaelovitch of Russia, by his morganatic wife, Countess Torby. Nada was brought up mainly in England where her parents lived at Keele Hall, Staffordshire, and then at Kenwood, Hampstead, which they rented from the Earl of Mansfield. She had an hypnotic quality attracting many female friends as well as men. Following her wedding to Prince George of Battenberg (later Lord Milford Haven) at the Chapel Royal, naval ratings from his ship towed the wedding car along the entire length of St. James's Street on its way to the reception. She and George were dedicated socialites of the 20s and 30s, being dubbed the 'seen abouters'. In 1932, he was described in a fashionable magazine as 'pale, slim, a gently cynical talker, first-rate judge, but not a heavy consumer of wine and food, a hardened cigarette smoker, wears diamond rings and flamboyant evening cuff-links – and gets away with it'; she, 'a Grand Duke's daughter, lightly greying hair, youthful face, large eyes and fond of black lace for evening frocks'. She lived in near seclusion following her husband's early death in 1938.

'Anyone for Tennis?' Queen Victoria Eugenie of Spain, her daughter Beatriz and Crown Prince Gustav Adolf of Sweden prepare for a game of tennis at Bagshot Park. One assumes that the Queen is merely holding the racquet in readiness for her daughter to play, as her suit and hat do not appear to give her much freedom of movement. It is interesting to note, that the two wives of Gustav Adolf, Margaret and Louise, were 1st cousins to the Queen of Spain.

Taken at Prinz Emil's Garden, Darmstadt, about 1908 by Princess Anna of Battenberg, showing from left to right: Princess Louis of Battenberg, her cousin, Princess Marie Louise of Schleswig-Holstein, her son, Prince Louis and her brother-in-law Prince Franz Joseph of Battenberg. The obscured figure is probably Princess Louise of Battenberg (daughter of Princess Louis). Young Louis has written on the reverse 'Mama, Louie Holstein, Self and Uncle Frazius'. Prince Franz Joseph was a Doctor of Philosophy who had married in 1897 Princess Anna, a daughter of the King of Montenegro. She died at the age of 96 in 1974 and, at that time, held the record for being the longest lived member, by birth, of a European royal house until Princess Alice, Countess of Athlone, beat that record by living to be almost 98 in 1981.

The setting for this photograph is the garden of Coppins, home of the Duke and Duchess of Kent, and it was taken in 1936 while the subjects are wearing mourning for King George V. It seems somewhat bizarre to see them in full mourning clothes and hats sitting on sunbeds and a Li-Lo. From the left: Princess Marie Louise, the Duchess of Kent with Prince Edward, now Duke of Kent, Lady Patricia Ramsay and Princess Helena Victoria.

Princess Beatrice with her granddaughter Infanta Maria Christina of Spain and Lady Patricia Ramsay at Brantridge Park, Balcombe, Sussex, during the late 1920s. As the Princess became more infirm, her Spanish descendants would visit her in England where she often stayed at the home of her niece, Princess Alice, Countess of Athlone. The Athlones were inveterate travellers and gave her free rein at Brantridge during their many absences.

The Duke of Connaught at Cowes with Lady Leslie, 1907. Lady Leslie was the sister of Lady Randolph Churchill and was born Leonie Jerome in America. For over four decades, she was a close companion of the duke and was also very friendly with the duchess, who fully approved of the situation. Leonie also got on well with the duke's children and grandchildren who realised she was a great support to him particularly as the duchess was neither robust or outgoing.

The Duchess of Connaught book-binding, Government House, Ottawa, 1915. The Duchess was beginning to suffer from a series of illnesses from which she never fully recovered. She was also a solitary woman who gained much pleasure from her hobby of book-binding. Many examples of her work still exist which display her skill and aptitude.

Prince and Princess Arthur of Connaught had a cottage at Virginia Water in Windsor Great Park, where Princess Arthur took this photograph about 1930. Princess Helena Victoria is peeking into the picture at the left, the Earl of Macduff appears to have just emerged from the lake, Prince Arthur sits in the boat while Lady Patricia Ramsay is still partly submerged. The Earl of Athlone partly draped with towelling is still wearing his town shoes and Colonel Fitzroy Fyers, an equerry to the Duke of Connaught, is discreetly covered in a long white towel while the Duke looks on in a bemused manner. The swimming parties continued up to the death of Prince Arthur in 1938 and were enjoyed by three generations of the Connaught family; the old Duke himself occasionally taking a dip.

◄ *A Grandson and Son of Queen Victoria, Prince Ernest, Grand Duke of Hesse, with his uncle, the Duke of Connaught, at a Military Parade in Germany, 1896. The Grand Duke was brother to Tsarina Alexandra of Russia and Grand Duchess Elizabeth of Russia, both of whom were despatched by the Bolsheviks in 1918. He was also great uncle of Prince Philip. Following his unhappy first marriage, he found lasting contentment with Princess Eleonore of Solms-Hohensolms-Lich, whom he married in 1905. A keen lover of the Arts, particularly music and painting, he was also a skilful engineer having invented an aeroplane which made many successful flights.*

Captain Alexander Ramsay of Mar. After the War, Sandy sent himself up to Oxford to study agriculture, qualifying as a land agent. For three years he worked for the Marquess of Linlithgow at Hopetoun House, outside Edinburgh, before starting his own land agents business in Easter Ross. He became Laird of Mar in 1959 when he was left the Mar Lodge Estate by his aunt, Princess Arthur of Connaught. Death duties at 80 per cent meant that much of the estate had to be sold though some land was retained where he and his wife, Flora, built a house which combines tradition and charm with comfort and practicality. In the summer of 2000, a party, which was attended by the Queen, was held there to celebrate his 80th and his wife's 70th birthdays. He became very involved in Scottish life being a Deputy Lieutenant for Aberdeenshire, Chairman of the Scottish Lifeboat Society and Patron of the Braemar Highland Gathering.

Taken by the author at Inverey House, Braemar, 2002. Lady Saltoun at the right with her second daughter, Alice, and her children, left to right: Victoria, George, Oliver and Alexander Ramsey. Having fought a vigorous campaign, Lady Saltoun was one of the 92 hereditary peers to remain in the House of Lords for an interim period where she speaks on a wide range of issues. As well as being a Peeress in her own right and head of the Name Fraser, she has written a history of the Clan Fraser, is an accomplished cook, does exquisite needlework and, arguably, makes the best dry martini in Aberdeenshire. She has three daughters, the eldest, Kate, will one day succeed as the 21st Lady Saltoun of Abernethy. Alice Ramsay upon marriage changed her surname by only one letter becoming Ramsey. The youngest daughter, Eliza, lives in London and was one of Queen Victoria's descendants to be included in a Country Life photograph, taken one hundred years after the Queen's death to emulate the Tuxen painting of the royal family at the time of the Golden Jubilee in 1887.

A pre-dinner photograph outside Shotton Hall, Shrewsbury, 1924. After his retirement from the Army in 1918, Adolphus, first Marquess of Cambridge and his wife, Meg, bought this house which was a haven for their family. Their younger son, Freddie, when not on army duties, lived there and Queen Mary often went to stay. The Prince of Wales was staying there in 1927 to open the New English Bridge at Shrewsbury when his uncle, Dolly, died suddenly. Left to right: the Duke of Beaufort, the Countess of Eltham, the Marchioness of Cambridge (Meg), the Earl of Eltham (later second Marquess of Cambridge), the Duchess of Beaufort and the Marquess of Cambridge (Dolly).

Colonel John Evelyn Gibbs at Sirinigar. Evie Gibbs, who was born in 1879 in London, was brought up in Victorian splendour at Tyntesfield, Somerset – a vast pile built by his grandfather from the profits of importing, amongst other things, guano. He became a regular soldier serving with the Coldstream Guards and was awarded the Military Cross in the First World War. For much of the War, he kept a detailed diary – and in an entry for 16th August 1914 he describes a train journey to Amiens in Northern France: 'the enthusiasm of the large crowds of people at every station, offering wine, cigars, cigarettes and bread, all accompanied by much singing of the Marseillaise, full of great jubilation that the British Army had come so soon'. By September 15th, he was in the thick of it, gunfire and shells all around, being awakened at 2 a.m. by heavy firing. He describes 90lb. shells exploding too close for comfort, with every C.O. in the first battalion either killed or wounded; eventually only one officer and fifty-one men survived. He came through the War unscathed, marrying Lady Helena Cambridge at St. George's Chapel, Windsor, in 1919.

52

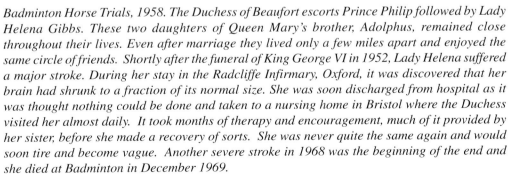

Badminton Horse Trials, 1958. The Duchess of Beaufort escorts Prince Philip followed by Lady Helena Gibbs. These two daughters of Queen Mary's brother, Adolphus, remained close throughout their lives. Even after marriage they lived only a few miles apart and enjoyed the same circle of friends. Shortly after the funeral of King George VI in 1952, Lady Helena suffered a major stroke. During her stay in the Radcliffe Infirmary, Oxford, it was discovered that her brain had shrunk to a fraction of its normal size. She was soon discharged from hospital as it was thought nothing could be done and taken to a nursing home in Bristol where the Duchess visited her almost daily. It took months of therapy and encouragement, much of it provided by her sister, before she made a recovery of sorts. She was never quite the same again and would soon tire and become vague. Another severe stroke in 1968 was the beginning of the end and she died at Badminton in December 1969.

The Duchess of Beaufort (centre) with King George V and Lady Westmorland at Sandringham, 1930. Mary Beaufort was a great favourite of the King. Unlike his children, she was not afraid of him; a characteristic he secretly admired. Because of the rapport between them she was regularly asked to Windsor, Sandringham and Balmoral where she would accompany the King on his shooting expeditions. He would allow her to borrow his horses without first asking, something his sons would not have dared do.

Princess Alice Countess of Athlone, aged 94, taken at Kensington Palace, with her great granddaughters, Katherine Abel Smith and Alice Liddell-Grainger. On the same day, Princess Alice was photographed with her four great grandsons. She refused to be taken with the boys and girls together, giving no reason and no amount of persuasive arguments would change her mind. Kate Abel Smith now lives in Ireland breeding horses and Alice Pannagio has lived in Italy for a number of years and is a successful designer of leather goods.

Whilst on leave from Africa, in the summer of 2002, Anne Grainger celebrated her 70th birthday with a tea party at Kensington Palace – the place of her birth. She is seen here in a photograph taken by the author on the steps of Clock House, which is where her christening photographs were taken. Her daughter Alice Pannagio sits next to her, flanked by Anne's four sons. From left, Charlie, Malcolm, Ian and Simon Liddell-Grainger.

The last visit Princess Alice made to her brother, the Duke of Albany and Saxe-Coburg and Gotha before the onset of World War One, was in 1913, to Gotha. Here, they attended an air show and are pictured watching a flying display. Left to right: Princess Alice with Prince Rupert of Teck, 'Charlie' Duke of Albany and Saxe-Coburg, Prince Philipp of Saxe-Coburg, 'Dick' Duchess of Albany and Saxe-Coburg, Frau von Wangenhiem, Prince Johann Leopold of Saxe-Coburg, unidentified man, Prince Alexander of Teck and Herr Wangenhiem. After 1914, it was to be seven years before brother and sister met and even then these occasions were infrequent. Not until the mid 1930s was the Duke of Coburg allowed to visit his native land, long after he had been deprived of his British styles and titles.

Lady May Cambridge with her mother, Princess Alice Countess of Athlone, at Waterloo Station about to return to South Africa in 1927. While this photograph was being taken, Lord Athlone was standing on the platform saying goodbye to various officials, when suddenly and without warning the train moved off at a fairly brisk pace. Athlone started to race along the platform and Princess Alice waved frantically for the train to stop, which it finally did reversing all the way into the station where the somewhat irate Earl quickly got on board.

Princess Alice Countess of Athlone in Saudi Arabia, 1938. A five day official visit was followed by a three week journey through the desert eventually arriving at the Persian Gulf. This exotic adventure took them through ancient settlements, nomadic encampments and endless sand dunes. For most of the journey she and her husband (next page) were ensconced in native dress. Sometimes the local food, which had to be eaten with appreciative relish, did not stay down too long. There were some discreet regurgitations which took place well away from the public gaze.

In characteristic gleeful mood, Princess Alice Countess of Athlone with Sir Geoffrey Hawkins, a fellow guest, at the wedding of Prince Richard of Gloucester, Barnwell Manor, 1972. Princess Alice had a well-honed sense of humour and loved to deflate pomposity. A new assistant butler was working for Princess Marina, a neighbour of Princess Alice at Kensington Palace. One morning, Marina fancied some bacon for breakfast and finding none in the fridge, the butler sent his assistant next door to Princess Alice's kitchen, where he encountered an elderly lady 'doing the flowers'. 'Marina fancies some bacon today dear, have you got a spare rasher?' She stopped what she was doing went to the larder emerging with two large rashers, 'hope she enjoys them, it's the best back' was her parting remark. A week later, Princess Marina announced that Princess Alice was coming to tea that day. The assistant butler, on opening the front door that afternoon, was astonished to find that his supposed cook was none other than 'Her Royal Highness'. With a furtive wink and twinkle in her eye, she whispered 'don't worry, it's our secret'. ▶

Lady May Abel Smith launching a tourist boat, Lake Burley Griffin, Canberra, Australia. Sir Henry was appointed Administrator of Australia during the lengthy absence of the Governor General which meant they had to move from Brisbane with its sultry days to the cooler climes of Australian Capital Territory. May, a rather shy, unassuming person, was catapulted from the more low-key duties and life as wife of a state governor to that of becoming Australia's First Lady, with all its attendant high profile engagements. She was never completely at ease in the limelight and it was an ordeal for her to attend countless receptions and make speeches – talking was never a problem for Lady May, making speeches was. Only once did her mask slip when she and Sir Henry had to eat in front of a large crowd some fried Witchetty Grubs; very large, fat wood maggots, which are prized as a great delicacy by Aboriginals.

Because of their popularity, Sir Henry Abel Smith's term of office as Governor of Queensland was increased from four to eight years. He worked to a punishing schedule, travelling the length and breadth of outback and coastal Queensland, often living in a train for several weeks. Her Lady-in-Waiting at the time recalled that as a visit to Birdsville, a remote town, was planned, the secretary wrote to enquire about any suitable cattle stations where they could rest and have a day off. Lady May chuckled for weeks over the reply: 'there are no suitable cattle stations within range, there is, however, an hotel which can offer unmolested accommodation'. The picture above shows the Abel Smiths on the ceremonial drive to Brisbane Airport on their return to England in 1966 and that, at the right, the enormous crowds who came to wish them 'Bon Voyage' as their procession made its way along Queen Street. An unprecedented scene and one never likely to be repeated.

To escape English winters, Princess Beatrice visited the Athlones in South Africa, where, although officially on holiday, she took part in public ceremonies. Here, resembling a 'Dreadnought', she leaves the Parliament Building in Cape Town following the State Opening by the Earl of Athlone. Beatrice would also visit her daughter, Queen Ena, in Spain until heart problems prevented her from visiting Madrid, where the high altitude was detrimental to her condition.

The Marchioness of Carisbrooke with Noel Coward at a charity gala in London, 1938. Irene Carisbrooke was a kind, gentle, hard-working member of the royal family. She particularly endeared herself to King George V and Queen Mary for her stoicism in the face of her husband's lack of conjugal interest. In 1919, two years after her marriage to Lord Carisbrooke, the King wrote to her following a lunch she had attended at Buckingham Palace; saying what an asset she was to his family, how they understood her problems and they would not breathe a word to anyone about what she had revealed. He went on to say that it only confirmed what they had long suspected. Her endless charity work continued unabated until just a few weeks before she died of cancer at 66 in 1956.

The Marquess of Carisbrooke (Drino) was mainly a businessman though he did support his wife's charitable endeavours. Following his retirement, he took on some of his wife's patronages and this charming photograph shows him with children with learning difficulties. As a young soldier based at St. James's Palace, he wrote a series of questionable letters to a young captain of the 1st Life Guards, who was also based in London, but at Knightsbridge Barracks. In one letter, dated 1910, when his friend failed to turn up, Drino expresses great disappointment, ending with 'I do want you dear thing and hate turning in after looking forward to meeting all day'. In another short note later that year, he writes 'I am coming in tonight to see you dear thing on my return, this day cannot pass without my seeing you'. Perhaps it is not surprising that King George and Queen Mary had long had their suspicions.

Princess Alice was always keen to encourage young people to be good, upright, responsible citizens. To this end, she actively supported the Cubs, Scouts, Brownies, Girl Guides, Sea Cadets and the like. She believed fervently in God, Queen and Country, feeling that if these beliefs were established at an early age, people would demonstrate a greater sense of care and concern for each other. She never talked down to children, unfailingly treating them as equals. She knew how to encourage the tongue-tied just as easily as dealing with the verbose, to whom she would chat with equal charm.

The last photograph of Princess Marie Louise taken 10 days before her death in December 1956. She was attending a Foyle's Literary Luncheon to launch her autobiography, 'My Memories of Six Reigns'. She claimed to have written every word in longhand using soft HB pencils. During her last few years, she had been close to death on more than one occasion, this, however, did not stop her from carrying on with the 'royal round'. A strict disciplinarian when it came to 'chairing a committee', she could bring a room of chattering women to attention with a clap of the hand and a raised eyebrow. At one committee meeting, her Lady-in-Waiting failed to pay attention and listen to the Princess: 'I'll do the talking Phyllis' she remarked sharply. Due to her heavy consumption of gin at the Queen's Coronation, her progress down the aisle of Westminster Abbey was somewhat erratic, pausing when she should have been walking. Her Lady-in-Waiting, the long-suffering Mrs. Murray, who had been trying to keep the required distance, trod on her train earning a sharp rebuke: 'you're a fool, Phyllis, you always were'. Whereupon the Princess grabbed her train, threw it over her left arm and marched unsteadily out of the Abbey.

◄

Princess Helena Victoria accompanied by Lady Patricia Ramsay at an official visit to a YMCA establishment, 1919. Known as Thora, she was a favourite grandchild of Queen Victoria and she spent much time with the Queen during her final weeks at Osborne, writing the Queen's journal entries for her as her strength and eyesight began to fail. Twenty-two days before she died, an entry in the Queen's journal reads 'at a little after nine after having my supper of Bengers food, Harriet P read to me, and I fell quite asleep so that Thora did not write the journal as it had got too late'. Thora was President of the YMCA National Women's Auxiliary Section, she was also President of the Princess Christian Nursing Home at Windsor, an establishment founded by her mother. Her last public appearance was in November 1947 at the wedding of the present Queen, where she is seen in the official group at Buckingham Palace seated in a wheelchair, her ever faithful sister, Princess Marie Louise, standing close by.

The Milford Havens visit the Maidenhead Fishery, 1931. Victoria, Marchioness of Milford Haven did not become regularly involved in public duties, unlike her son George and his wife Nada, although their public appearances tended to lean towards events of a social nature: charity balls, dinner parties, charity auctions and race meetings were their preferred territory. George Milford Haven took a great part in the upbringing of his nephew Prince Philip of Greece following the disintegration of his parental home in 1931. His mother, in a sanitorium, his sisters had all married and lived abroad and his father had decamped to the South of France. His education and holidays were supervised by Uncle George and Aunt Nada and, although much has been made of the part Lord Mountbatten played in Prince Philip's early life, by the time of George Milford Haven's death in 1938, Philip was already 17 and at naval college. From the left: the Marchioness of Milford Haven (Nada), her daughter Lady Tatiana Mountbatten, the Marquess of Milford Haven (George), Prince Philip, the Dowager Marchioness of Milford Haven (Victoria) and Count Michael Torby (Boy), brother of Nada.

Princess Victoria Melita of Edinburgh, Grand Duchess of Hesse, with her daughter, Princess Elizabeth of Hesse. It was at Victoria's wedding in Coburg in 1894, which was attended by Queen Victoria, the Kaiser and a host of European royalty that Princess Alexandra of Hesse (sister of the groom) became engaged to Nicholas the Russian Tsarevitch. They became Emperor and Empress later that year having married at St. Petersburg barely three weeks after the death of Tsar Alexander III. The facts of their ghastly end at the hands of the Bolsheviks are too well documented to need repeating.

A brother-in-law of Prince Philip, Prince Gottfried of Hohenlohe-Langenburg with his parents Prince Ernst and Princess Alexandra, 1897. Prince Philip and his four sisters are, through their mother, Princess Alice of Battenberg, great great grandchildren of Queen Victoria. With the exception of Princess Theodora, all married amongst the Queen's many descendants. Margarita, the eldest sister, married Prince Gottfried (pictured). Princess Cecile became the wife of George Donatus, Hereditary Grand Duke of Hesse (a great grandson through Princess Alice, Queen Victoria's third child) and was killed with him, their two sons and her mother-in-law in an air crash near Ostend in 1937. Philip's youngest sister Sophie was married to two German princes, both of whom were descended from Queen Victoria's eldest child, the Empress Frederick. She married firstly in 1930 Prince Christopher of Hesse, who was killed in action in the Apennines in 1943, leaving her with four children, a fifth being born four months later. She married again, in 1946, Prince Georg of Hanover by whom she had a further three children. Princess Sophie was the last of Prince Philip's sisters to die (2001). Prince Georg is still alive at the time of writing.

The mother of Princess Marina, Duchess of Kent, Grand Duchess Helen Vladimirovna of Russia at left, with her mother, Grand Duchess Marie Pavlovna of Russia. Helen was very conscious of being born an Imperial Highness and a Grand Duchess of Russia and, as such, required 'Her Due'. When she married into the less exalted and more relaxed royal house of Greece, she tended to look down on her sisters-in-law, who she believed were from far less grand families than her own. She passed on some of these attitudes to her daughter Marina, who in turn was very proud of her long, royal ancestry, expecting people to know their place.

Born a Princess of Hanover and Great Britain and Ireland, Princess Frederika was the daughter of the last King of Hanover, the blind King George V. She fell in love with an ADC to her father, Baron von Pawel-Rammingen; but as they were of unequal rank, it would have been social death to marry and remain in Germany. Queen Victoria had no such scruples concerning rank or style and she allowed them to marry at Windsor in the Private Chapel of the Castle. She also gave them an apartment at Hampton Court Palace and when an infant daughter died, she allowed the remains to be placed in the Royal Vault at St. George's Chapel. Frederika, who was known within the family as cousin Lily, and the Baron, eventually went to live at Biarritz, where he died in 1932 and was buried there. Frederika had died in 1926, aged 78, and, by the express permission of King George V, she was reunited with her daughter, Victoria, in the Royal Vault at Windsor. It was in the Rammingen's house in Biarritz that Princess Victoria Eugenie of Battenberg took instruction in the Roman Catholic faith prior to marrying King Alfonso of Spain in 1906.

Charles Edward, Duke of Saxe-Coburg, at left, and his wife Victoria Adelheid, with two of his cousins, sons of the German Emperor: Prince August Wilhelm, left, and Prince Oscar. August Wilhelm who was known 'Auwi', married in 1908 a sister of the Duchess of Coburg, Princess Alexandra of Schleswig-Holstein-Glucksburg, and it was she who took this photograph. The marriage was not a success and they were divorced in 1920. Her second marriage to a commoner also ended in divorce and she finally lived in a caravan near Wiesbaden making a living from painting portraits and landscapes.

Victoria Adelheid, Duchess of Saxe-Coburg, with the head keeper's wife at Hinterris, Austria, 1969. After the deprivations she suffered following the War and the death of her husband in 1954, the old Duchess enjoyed a golden sunset. A frequent visitor to England to stay with her sister-in-law, Princess Alice Countess of Athlone, she attended family weddings here and, one year, she appeared on the balcony of Buckingham Palace at the Sovereign's Birthday Parade. She also visited her daughter Sibylla at the Swedish Court and had the satisfaction of knowing that one day her grandson would become King of Sweden. She died in 1970 at Grein in Upper Austria where her funeral took place, after which her remains were transferred to Coburg to lie in a little plot in a wooded glade at Callenberg, in a grave next to her husband Charlie and son Hubertus, who was killed in Russia in 1943 when his aeroplane was shot down.

Princess Caroline Mathilde of Saxe-Coburg with her fiancé Count Friedrich Wolfgang zu Castell-Rudenhausen, 1931. Considered fast by some of her more traditional relatives, Caroline Mathilde was married three times and had numerous lovers. Her first husband, whom she divorced in 1938, was killed in action over Dorset in 1940. Captain Max Schnirring of the German Air Force was her second husband. He too died as a result of the War in 1944. As a widow with six children, the youngest only eighteen months old, she had to take on a number of jobs to provide for the needs of a growing family. She married for the last time, in 1946, Karl Andree, a union which ended in divorce twelve months later. Caroline Mathilde was one of those German royals who lost their status as a Princess of Great Britain and Ireland in 1917.

Mr. and Mrs. Miles Huntington-Whiteley, taken by the author in Prince of Wales Court, Kensington Palace, 1997. Born Countess Victoria zu Castell-Rudenhausen at Coburg in 1935, she is the eldest daughter of Caroline Mathilde. Much of her childhood was spent with her Coburg grandparents travelling to one or another of their seven castles. When she was 21, she came to London, being taken under the wing of her great aunt Princess Alice Countess of Athlone, living with her at Kensington Palace. As a student nurse at St. Thomas's Hospital she was known simply as Nurse Castell, as she felt that patients would be put off if they knew of her long and complicated title. When her wedding to Miles Huntington-Whiteley took place at the Queen's Chapel, St. James's Palace in 1960, the 'low papers' made much of the fact that she was the first German to marry there since pre-1914 days. Her husband, as well as being a nephew of Rudyard Kipling, is the grandson of Stanley Baldwin, the Prime Minister at the centre of the Abdication crisis. At the 1972 Birthday Parade, the newly-widowed Duchess of Windsor was staying at Buckingham Palace where she was pictured looking through a window at the Parade below. A few yards away, on the Palace balcony, surrounded by the royal family stood the young Louise Huntington-Whiteley, great grand-daughter of Stanley Baldwin. One wonders what thoughts might have gone through the Duchess's mind had she realised she was so close to a descendant of the man who had taken one of the leading roles in the Abdication of her husband. Victoria Huntington-Whiteley is very much involved with charitable work and she often accompanies invalids to Lourdes, under the auspices of the Order of St. John of Jerusalem.

Three first cousins of Prince Philip with their children, Villa Malbosc, Grasse, 1951. The Duchess of Kent and Princess Olga of Yugoslavia with Princess Eugenie of Greece and her second husband Prince Raymond Della Torre e Tasso. Princess Eugenie, the daughter of Prince George of Greece and Princess Marie Bonaparte, was a woman of high intellect who wrote scholarly biographies of her great great grandfather Prince Lucien Bonaparte (Napoleon's younger brother) and her great grandfather Prince Pierre Napoleon Bonaparte. Brought up in France and partly reared on donkey's milk, she had a comfortable childhood, her mother's grandfather being the proprietor of the Monte Carlo Casino, Francois Blanc. She divorced both husbands, Prince Dominic Radziwill in 1946 and Prince Raymond in 1965. Her last years were clouded by Alzheimer's disease. Left to right: Prince Raymond Della Torre e Tasso, Prince Michael of Kent, Prince George Radziwill and Princess Tatiana Radziwill (the children of Eugenie), Princess Alexandra of Kent, the Duchess of Kent, Princess Eugenie (standing), the Duke of Kent and Princesses Olga and Elizabeth of Yugoslavia.

Princess Olga of Yugoslavia with four of her grandchildren. She was the eldest sister of Princess Marina Duchess of Kent, to whom she was a great support when the Duke of Kent was killed in 1942. King George VI removed in superable obstacles to allow Olga to travel to England in the middle of the War. She and Prince Paul settled in Italy in 1948 to be near her cousins, Queen Helen of Roumania and Princess Irene Duchess Aosta, who lived at Fiesole, just outside Florence. Olga often came to London staying with Marina and, following her death, she would stay in another apartment at Kensington Palance, that of Princess Alice Countess of Athlone. She could be a demanding guest; Princess Alice and her small staff did not relish those visits. After Princess Alice died she would then stay at Clarence House with Queen Elizabeth the Queen Mother, and failing any other accommodation, she would decamp to Claridges where she received her royal relations and the Yugoslav community with equal warmth. She is pictured in the 1960s accompanied by the twins, Prince Dimitri (left) and Prince Michel of Yugoslavia, who are holding the hands of their sister, Princess Helen. She is carrying her granddaughter Catherine Oxenberg.

Princess Theodora, the second sister of Prince Philip, is pictured (second left) with her husband, Berthold, the Margrave of Baden, and their children, Max (left), Ludwig and Margarita. As a 16 year old, Princess Margarita came to live in London, training to be a nurse; a profession she worked at for many years. She stayed firstly with her great grandmother, the Dowager Marchioness of Milford Haven at Kensington Palace. The old lady either did not feel the cold or was rather frugal as her apartment was frigid; so much so that Margarita would frequently walk to Barkers to do her studies in the warmth of the coffee shop.

Following the assassination of her husband King Alexander I in 1934 at Marseilles by a Macedonian terrorist, Queen Marie of Yugoslavia became a frequent visitor to England, where her two younger sons were at school. In 1938, she came to convalesce here after a serious operation and decided to settle; living firstly in Chelsea and later in Huntingdonshire and Surrey. She had been educated at Heathfield in Berkshire where she developed a great love of the English countryside. In exile she never forgot the Yugoslav people, devoting her time in the War to the task of supplying parcels to Yugoslav prisoners of war in Germany and Italy. At Clarence House, loyal Yugoslav helpers packed parcels under the encouraging eye of Queen Marie who drove to London almost daily, ignoring the constant bombing. When she died in London in 1961, at the age of 61, three thousand exiled Yugoslavs stood in torrential rain outside the Serbian Church, Ladbroke Grove, listening to the service which was broadcast over loudspeakers. In her will, she left three thousand pounds on trust for the benefit of Yugoslavs settled in England. She is buried at Frogmore, her stone simply states 'Marie, Queen of Yugoslavia born 1900 Gotha died 1961 London'. Queen Marie is here seen at Salem, Germany, in 1957, with the young King Simeon of Bulgaria and the Margrave of Baden (right), whose daughter Princess Margarita was about to marry her son Prince Tomislav. ▶

Prince Ludwig of Baden with his wife Princess Marianne of Auersperg-Breunner and their children, Aglae (left), Berthold and Sophie. Ludwig is a godson of Prince Philip and attended his old school Gordonstoun. He and his wife are guests each year of the Queen and Prince Philip for the Windsor Horse Show and also for a winter shooting party at Sandringham. He has a dry sense of humour and, unlike some members of German royal families, he is down to earth and relaxed. She is most stylish and very warm-hearted – a delightful couple.

▶

Princess Margarita of Baden (centre) with her brother the Margrave and his wife, Valerie, who is a direct descendant of the Emperor Franz Joseph of Austria, taken by the author, 1998, before the wedding of the Hon. Timothy Knatchbull. The Margrave (Max), assisted by his elder son Bernhard, runs their large estate at Salem on Lake Constance in Southern Germany. Princess Margarita is closely involved with plans to restore to full working order, the medical facilities of the Martha and Mary Convent in Moscow, which was founded by her great great aunt Grand Duchess Elizabeth of Russia.

The confirmation of Prince Ludwig of Baden and his cousin, Prince Karl of Hesse, at Salem, 1951. Back row: Prince Richard of Hesse, Prince Georg Wilhelm of Hanover, Prince Karl of Hesse, Prince Ludwig of Baden, Margrave Berthold of Baden, Princess Margarita of Baden, Prince Max of Baden and Princess Christina of Hesse. Middle row: Prince Rainer of Hesse, Princess Sophie of Hanover holding her son, the infant Prince Georg, and Margravine Theodora of Baden. Seated: Grand Duchess Alexandra of Mecklenburg-Schwerin, Princess Alice of Greece holding Prince Welf of Hanover, Landgravine Margarete of Hesse, Princess Clarissa of Hesse and Princess Olga of Hanover.

The 'Pimlico Princesses' 1956. Dubbed the 'Pimlico Princesses' by the British press, Princess Beatrix of Hohenlohe-Langenburg (left) and Princess Christina of Hesse, nieces of Prince Philip, took a ten pound a week flat in Rodney House, Dolphin Square, which their uncle helped to furnish from surplus items at Windsor. Beatrix was in London to study advanced dressmaking and Christina restoration of old master paintings. Stories of 'bohemian bottle parties' and of a general cavorting around filtered back to Langenburg, where Beatrix's parents were not amused, resulting in her peremptory return to Germany, a mere seven months after she had arrived here. Princess Christina meanwhile married a cousin, Prince Andrej of Yugoslavia. The Princesses are photographed with David Hicks enjoying a shooting range at the London Ball at the Savoy Hotel.

King Constantine of the Hellenes looks on as the coffin of his cousin Prince Peter of Greece is driven slowly away from the Greek Cathedral, Moscow Road, London, 1980. The King's aunt, Lady Katherine Brandram stands next to him, linking arms with Princess Eugenie, the sister of Prince Peter. After her marriage in 1947 to an English army officer, Princess Katherine was granted by King George VI the style of a duke's daughter and, since that time, has been known in this country as Lady Katherine Brandram. Although during the days when the Greek King was on the throne, she was always known as HRH Princess Katherine in Athens, being given her place as the daughter, sister and aunt of kings. She is one of the three surviving great grand-children of Queen Victoria.

Members of Europe's royal houses gather at Fredensborg for the Silver Wedding celebrations of King Frederick IX and Queen Ingrid of Denmark, 1960. Standing in front, Alexandra, Grand Duchess of Mecklenburg-Schwerin. Bottom step, left to right: Princess Margaretha of Sweden, Crown Princess Margrethe of Denmark, Queen Ingrid, King Frederik, Princess Dagmar of Denmark (Mrs. Castenskiold) and King Olav of Norway. Second row: Queen Louise and Princess Sibylla of Sweden, Princesses Anne-Marie and Benedikte of Denmark, King Gustav VI Adolf of Sweden, Princess Kira of Prussia and Princess Astrid of Norway. Third row: Duchess Thyra of Mecklenburg-Schwerin, Lady Patricia Ramsay, Grand Duchess Josephine Charlotte of Luxembourg, Princess Margethe of Bourbon Parma, Prince Axel, Prince Georg, Princess Anne, Princess Viggo and Princess Margaretha – all of Denmark. Fourth row: Arveprincess Caroline Mathilde of Denmark, Grand Duke Jean of Luxembourg, Prince Louis Ferdinand of Prussia, Princess Elizabeth of Denmark, Admiral the Hon. Sir Alexander Ramsay, Countess Ruth of Rosenborg, Count Flemming of Rosenborg and Duke Christian Ludwig of Mecklenburg-Schwerin. At rear: Jorgen Castenskiold and Prince Viggo of Denmark.

The Danish Silver Wedding day was to have been celebrated with a garden party at Fredensborg Castle, but torrential rain put an end to that. Apart from a fine spell when the large group photograph was taken, it rained incessantly, forcing the party to take place indoors where these photographs were taken. Close relatives of the couple gather before lunch, left to right: Princess Louis Ferdinand of Prussia, who was born a Princess of Russia, daughter of Grand Duke Kirill of Russia and his English wife Victoria Melita of Edinburgh. Her husband, Louis Ferdinand was a first cousin of King Frederick. His mother, Crown Princess Cecile of Prussia, being a sister of Queen Alexandrine of Denmark. Lady Patricia and Admiral the Hon. Alexander Ramsay, the aunt and uncle of Queen Ingrid, and Jorgen Castenskiold with his wife Princess Dagmar, the King's aunt. Right: Queen Louise of Sweden with Admiral Ramsay. The Ramsays were often in Denmark and Sweden visiting the descendants of her late sister Crown Princess Margaret of Sweden. They would always be at London airport to greet Queen Ingrid and her daughters on their many private visits to this country.

Queen Victoria Eugenie, surrounded by her many grandchildren in a group taken c. 1945. The Queen holds Donna Olimpia Torlonia, younger daughter of Infanta Beatriz. Olimpia's daughter, Sibilla Weiller, married, in 1994, Prince Guillame, a brother of Grand Duke Henri of Luxembourg. To the right of the Queen stands Infante Alfonso, a son of the Count of Barcelona and younger brother of King Juan Carlos, who died as the result of a shooting accident when he was 14. Standing, left to right: Don Marco Torlonia, Infante Juan Carlos (now King of Spain), Don Gonzalo (younger son of the Duke of Segovia, who was the second son of Queen Ena), Infanta Pilar (sister of the present King), Don Alfonso (elder son of the Duke of Segovia), he married a granddaughter of General Franco, Maria del Carmen, whereupon the General gave him the title, Duke of Cadiz, with the style of Royal Highness. He met an untimely end in Colorado in 1989 when, while skiing, he hit an overhead cable. Donna Sandra Torlonia, who caused a scandal when in 1958 she married secretly a thirty-two year old widower, Count Clemente Lequio, who gave his profession as 'office clerk'. At 6.50 a.m. Sandra, in a white shantung suit, with the bridegroom and two lawyers, knocked at the side door of the tiny Church of San Biagio in Rome. At 7 o'clock they were lead to the High Altar for a Nuptual Mass, after which they left in a cream coloured sports car driving south to the Amalfi Coast for a honeymoon. Sitting: Don Marino Torlonia, Infanta Margarita (the youngest sister of King Juan Carlos), who has suffered from tunnel vision all her life. While she can see a little, she always has to be guided, a task her husband, Doctor Juan Zurita y Delgado, performs with great devotion. And Donna Vittoria Marone and Donna Giovanna Marone (the two eldest daughters of Ena's daughter Infanta Maria Christina and her husband, Count Enrico Marone of the Cinzano drinks family).

Queen Victoria Eugenie of Spain bought a house at Lausanne, Switzerland, in 1949, where this photograph was taken. Her many visits to Britain always included staying with her brother Lord Carisbrooke in his Kensington Palace apartment. She would then move across the courtyard to stay with her cousin Princess Alice Countess of Athlone. Since being exiled in 1931, she returned only once to Spain when in 1968 she attended the christening of her great grandson, Prince Felipe. At the Queen's wedding reception at Buckingham Palace in 1947, Winston Churchill, looking her straight in the eye, asked 'have you been to Spain recently?' Retaining a dignified demeanour, she replied 'no, I never use the back door, I always arrive by the main entrance'.

Neu Strelitz 1912. The 90th Birthday of PrincessAugusta, Grand Duchess of Mecklenburg-Strelitz. Princess Augusta Caroline of Cambridge, aunt of Queen Mary, had married at Buckingham Palace in 1843 her first cousin the Grand Duke of Mecklenburg-Strelitz. The Grand Ducal Court, if small, was extremely stiff and formal so much so that there was little contact between parents and children who were completely hedged in by tutors and governesses. Augusta's surviving son, Adolphus, was married with two daughters and two sons. The elder daughter Duchess Marie who had lived a life sheltered from the realities of the outside world and was totally ignorant of the facts of life, was found at 19 to be heavily pregnant: a condition which seemed to have escaped her mother's notice. The culprit was a young married footman, one of whose duties was to carry the lamps into the rooms of the young duchesses. He was dismissed on the grounds of stealing and not given a reference, whereupon he leaked his story to the anti-monarchical press in Berlin. The poor girl was disowned by her parents who sent her to the South of France where she was joined by her grandmother Augusta. May, the Duchess of York, also arrived to lend her support. Marie married in 1899 Count Jametel – a French Papal Count – who was many years her senior and an opportunist who went through her money before she divorced him in 1908. Her second marriage to a Prince of Lippe was a very happy one. The younger granddaughter of Grand Duchess Augusta, Jutta was married in 1899 to Crown Prince Danilo of Montenegro and took the name of 'Militza'. Danilo assumed the title of King upon the death of his father on 1st March 1921; he abdicated six days later in favour of his nephew, Prince Michael. Standing: Grand Duke Adolphus of Mecklenburg-Strelitz (son of Augusta) with his son Duke Adolf Friedrich. Seated: Duchess Marie, Countess Jametel; Grand Duchess Elizabeth of Mecklenburg-Strelitz (daughter-in-law of Augusta); Augusta, Grand Duchess of Mecklenburg-Strelitz; Jutta (Militza), Crown Princess of Montenegro. At front: Countess Marie von Nemerow, a daughter of Duchess Marie.

The Silver Wedding of Princess Mary Adelaide, Duchess of Teck, and the Duke of Teck, White Lodge, Richmond Park, 1891. Left to right: Prince Francis of Teck, Mary Adelaide, the Duke of Teck (in front), Prince Alexander of Teck (later Earl of Athlone), Princess May of Teck (later Queen Mary) and Prince Adolphus of Teck (later Marquess of Cambridge). Princess Mary Adelaide of Cambridge was born in 1833 in Hanover during the time her father, the first Duke of Cambridge, was Viceroy. She was always rather stout; her mother despaired that she would ever marry a suitable prince. Finally, in 1866, at an age when it was considered that she might be left a spinster, she married an impoverished German princeling of morganatic descent, Franz Prince of Teck. In 1871 Franz was granted the title, Duke of Teck, by his kinsman King Wilhelm I of Wurttemberg and in 1887 Queen Victoria gave him the style of Highness out of gratitude for marrying 'Fat Mary'. An extremely approachable and warm-hearted woman she endeared herself to the working classes of London, being especially popular in the East End where she carried out numerous official engagements. Her public standing often exceeded that of the Queen and she was proclaimed 'the People's Princess' long before the much more famous wife of her great great grandson Charles, Prince of Wales. By the 1890s, Mary had grown so stout that when staying at Hopetoun House outside Edinburgh the doors there had to be widened so as to allow her free passage in a dignified manner.

The 2nd Duke of Cambridge as Field Marshal and Commander-in-Chief of the Army, c.1890s. A grandson of King George III and only son of Adolphus Duke of Cambridge, he was born in 1819 being two months older than his cousin, Queen Victoria. His early promise and active service in the Army culminated in him being appointed Commander-in-Chief. With the advance of years he became somewhat of a martinet, vigorously opposing any reforms or modern developments. Not long before he died in 1904, he almost had an apoplectic fit when his nephew, Prince Alexander of Teck arrived to see him, driving 'one of those damned infernal new-fangled motorcars'.

On the day of Queen Victoria's Wedding in 1840, according to his diary, the Duke of Cambridge met his future wife, the actress Louisa Fairbrother. A woman of great beauty she and the Duke married in secret and in contravention of the Royal Marriages Act, at St. John's Church, Clerkenwell, in 1847. They had three sons, George, Adolphus and Augustus, who bore the surname, FitzGeorge. Louisa adopted the pseudonym Mrs. FitzGeorge. They were a devoted couple, living as husband and wife at 6 Queen Street, Mayfair, in the evenings and off-duty days. He lived 'officially' at nearby Gloucester House, Piccadilly, which is now the site of the 'Hard Rock Cafe'. The Duke realised that his wife would be denied a burial in the Royal Vault at Windsor and so to ensure that they rested together he built a mausoleum at Kensal Green Cemetery where they lie with their two younger sons and other descendants. The Duke is photographed at Bad Homburg seated, with from left, Mrs. Louisa Hamilton, and his younger sons, Rear Admiral Sir Adolphus FitzGeorge and Colonel Sir Augustus FitzGeorge. It is possible that Louisa Hamilton was the daughter of the Duke and Mrs. FitzGeorge although she was never acknowledged as such. She was born in March 1841, a year after the Duke and Louisa first met. At her wedding to Captain Francis Hamilton in 1859, her surname on the marriage certificate was FitzGeorge and her father was named as George FitzGeorge and she was also present at the Duke's deathbed.

Colonel Sir Augustus FitzGeorge, the youngest son of the Duke of the Cambridge, never married. He inherited 6 Queen Street, Mayfair, where he entertained numerous lady friends. He had served in Tel-El-Kebir in 1882, was an A.D.C. to his father and at one time acted as his private secretary. He was Chairman of the General Committee of the Royal Cambridge Home for Soldiers' Widows. He and his brothers were received by Queen Victoria on a number of occasions; it is not certain if Queen Victoria ever met their mother. After his death, his niece Iris along with the Marchioness of Cambridge went to his house to collect some items of Cambridge family jewels, only to find the safe open and empty; his mistress having got there before them.

George FitzGeorge was the eldest son of the Duke and Mrs. FitzGeorge and is a rather shadowy figure; even his descendants know little about him except that he married Rosa Baring of the banking family and was a Colonel in the Welch Fusilliers, having served in the Egyptian campaign at Tel-El-Kebir. He seems to have been somewhat impecunious, the Duke from time to time paying off his debts. George was never particularly robust. At his father's funeral, unlike his brothers, he was not strong enough to walk behind the gun carriage from Westminster Abbey to Kensal Green Cemetery; having instead to ride in a carriage. He eventually lived largely abroad where he died in Switzerland in 1907, aged 54. His son, George FitzGeorge, married as his second wife a daughter of a French senateur, France Bellanger who was murdered in Paris.

The eldest child of George FitzGeorge, Iris, is photographed at her wedding to Robert Balfour in 1912. Iris, a close friend of Queen Mary, was granted certain privileges as a relation of the Royal Family. Not only was she married at the Chapel Royal, St. James's Palace, but her funeral also took place there. She was a trustee of The Royal Cambridge Home for Soldiers' Widows and occasionally she represented Princess Alice Countess of Athlone at memorial services. Following the death of her husband, she married Prince Vladimir Galitzine, an event which prompted Princess Alice to remark, 'well she's finally become a princess, it's what she always wanted to be'.

General Sir Victor FitzGeorge-Balfour's wife, Mary Diana Christian, was a descendant of ancient Manx landowners and related to Fletcher Christian of The Bounty.

Diana FitzGeorge-Balfour taken by the author in his apartment, 2002. A goddaughter of Queen Mary and only daughter of Sir Victor FitzGeorge-Balfour, Diana has continued the family's close association with the Cambridge Home for Soldiers' Widows where she is a trustee and a regular supporter of events held at the home in Molesey, Surrey. She is an aknowledgeable family historian.

General Sir Victor FitzGeorge-Balfour was the son of Iris FitzGeorge and a godson of Queen Mary and had an immensely distinguished career in the Army. His many appointments included that of Brigadier at the very early age of 28, Chief of Staff to the Governor of Cyprus, Lord Harding, Director of Military Operations at the Ministry of Defence, Vice-Chief of the General Staff and A.D.C. to the Queen. He was awarded an MC in Palestine in 1939 and DSO in Malaya in 1950. He was the first British Officer to see the horrors of Belsen when he was taken blind-folded into the Camp prior to its handover by the German authorities. His final posting was to Brussels as U.K. Military Adviser to NATO. In order to inherit family chattels from his great uncles Adolphus and Augustus, he was required to adopt FitzGeorge as part of his surname. An inveterate traveller, during his retirement he visited China before it was open to tourists, Easter Island and other remote locations

Robin FitzGeorge-Balfour with his wife Patricia who is from Mississippi. He is the only son of Victor and Mary FitzGeorge-Balfour and met his wife when they were students at Durham University. Like his father he became a Coldstreamer and is an investment broker in the city. He has worked in Hong Kong where his younger son, Victor, was born. They have two daughters, Charlotte (left) and Sophie. And two sons, Victor (left) and George.

FitzGeorge

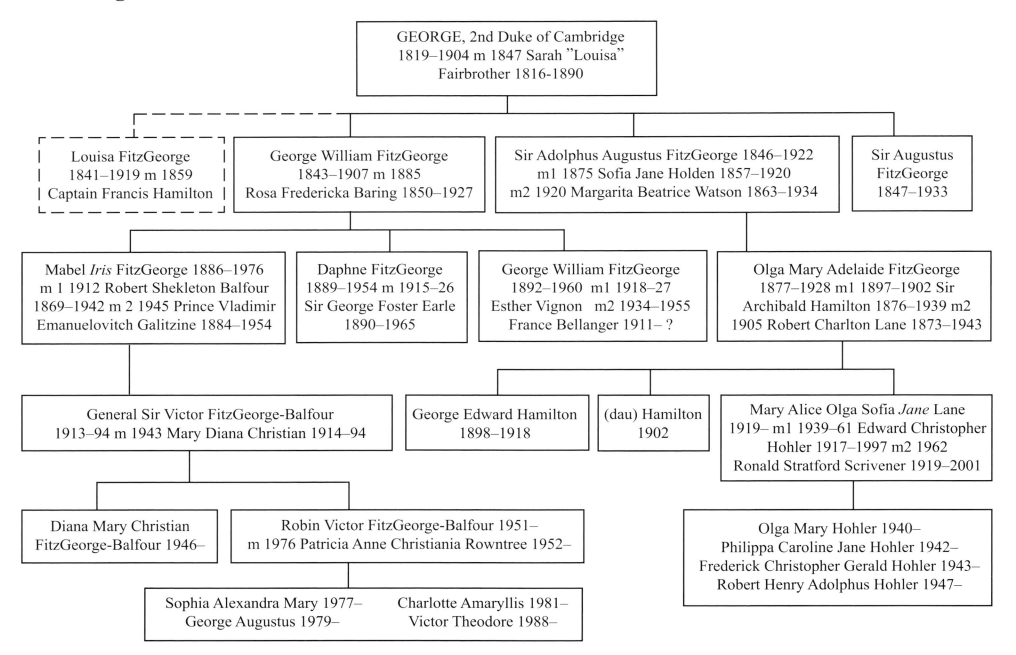

GEORGE, 2nd Duke of Cambridge
1819–1904 m 1847 Sarah "Louisa"
Fairbrother 1816-1890

Louisa FitzGeorge
1841–1919 m 1859
Captain Francis Hamilton

George William FitzGeorge
1843–1907 m 1885
Rosa Fredericka Baring 1850–1927

Sir Adolphus Augustus FitzGeorge 1846–1922
m1 1875 Sofia Jane Holden 1857–1920
m2 1920 Margarita Beatrice Watson 1863–1934

Sir Augustus
FitzGeorge
1847–1933

Mabel *Iris* FitzGeorge 1886–1976
m 1 1912 Robert Shekleton Balfour
1869–1942 m 2 1945 Prince Vladimir
Emanuelovitch Galitzine 1884–1954

Daphne FitzGeorge
1889–1954 m 1915–26
Sir George Foster Earle
1890–1965

George William FitzGeorge
1892–1960 m1 1918–27
Esther Vignon   m2 1934–1955
France Bellanger 1911– ?

Olga Mary Adelaide FitzGeorge
1877–1928 m1 1897–1902 Sir
Archibald Hamilton 1876–1939 m2
1905 Robert Charlton Lane 1873–1943

General Sir Victor FitzGeorge-Balfour
1913–94 m 1943 Mary Diana Christian 1914–94

George Edward Hamilton
1898–1918

(dau) Hamilton
1902

Mary Alice Olga Sofia *Jane* Lane
1919– m1 1939–61 Edward Christopher
Hohler 1917–1997 m2 1962
Ronald Stratford Scrivener 1919–2001

Diana Mary Christian
FitzGeorge-Balfour 1946–

Robin Victor FitzGeorge-Balfour 1951–
m 1976 Patricia Anne Christiania Rowntree 1952–

Olga Mary Hohler 1940–
Philippa Caroline Jane Hohler 1942–
Frederick Christopher Gerald Hohler 1943–
Robert Henry Adolphus Hohler 1947–

Sophia Alexandra Mary 1977–
George Augustus 1979–

Charlotte Amaryllis 1981–
Victor Theodore 1988–

Four generations. The Duke of Cambridge is photographed with his son, Adolphus, and granddaughter Olga with her son, George, by her first husband George Hamilton. Young George was killed in action in 1918 aged 19. Sir Adolphus FitzGeorge was married twice. His second wife, Margarita, outlived him and on her death in 1934, Queen Mary, who had once visited their house in Eccleston Square, sent a letter to her nephew Lord Cambridge, who was a neighbour of Lady FitzGeorge, asking him to obtain 'cheaply' various family pictures before they went to auction. Her note was quite precise as to the exact location in the house of each picture she wished to buy. On the right, George Edward Archibald Augustus FitzGeorge Hamilton – a photograph from the album of his grandfather Adolphus. His godparents, who attended in person at his christening at The Chapel Royal, St James's Palace, included King George V, Queen Mary and the Duke of Cambridge.

The marriage of Jane Lane and Edward Christopher Hohler, 1939. They had two sons and two daughters. Jane is the last surviving great grandchild of the Duke of Cambridge.

Olga FitzGeorge was divorced from Edward Hamilton in 1902, marrying three years later Squadron Leader Robert Lane. Fourteen years later she gave birth to a daughter, Jane Lane, and died when Jane was only nine years old.

Mrs Jane Scrivener taken by the author at a FitzGeorge exhibition, Kensal Green Cemetery, 2000. Her second husband, Ronald Scrivener, was a diplomat and they spent several years in Bangkok and Panama. He became Ambassador to Czechoslovakia where they lived in the superb embassy building in Prague. He was appointed a Companion of the Order of St Michael & St George, dying in 2001.

Royal guests assemble at Windsor Castle for the wedding in 1905 of Princess Margaret of Connaught and Prince Gustav Adolf of Sweden. Left to right: the Princess Royal Duchess of Fife, Crown Princess Victoria of Sweden, Queen Alexandra, Crown Prince Gustav of Sweden, Princess Victoria, and Prince Wilhelm of Sweden, who was best man for his brother. Wilhelm married Grand Duchess Maria Pavlovna (the younger) of Russia, who was a great-niece of Queen Alexandra and also a niece of Marie, Duchess of Edinburgh. Queen Alexandra wears the Diadem which had been made for the Coronation of King George IV, and which is now worn each year by the Queen on her way to and from the State Opening of Parliament.

*Grand Duchess Eliza-
beth of Mecklenburg-
Strelitz. Born a of Prin-
cess of Anhalt, a minor
German state, Eliza-
beth married Adolphus,
son of Grand Duchess
Augusta, who in turn
became Grand Duke on
his father's death in
1904. She loved to wear
expensive gowns and
jewellery: soon after be-
coming Grand Duchess
her mother-in-law in
typical waspish manner
wrote to Queen Mary
that 'Elly was revelling
in her new position,
wearing a new Parisian
gown every day and
the most elaborate je-
wellery, even when di-
ning en famille'.*

*Princess Augusta, Grand Duchess of Mecklenburg-Strelitz in the robes she wore at the coronation
of King Edward VII, 1902. At this time she was one of the few survivors who remembered the
coronations of William IV and Queen Victoria and as such, her advice was sought on certain
details of the ceremonial. As part of her robes she wears a Kirtle and her coronet is that of a
British Princess. At her wrists she wears the Family Order of King William IV and, on her robes,
she wears the Family Order of King George IV and the order of the Crown of India.*

The Duchess of Albany in 1902, dressed for the Coronation of King Edward VII. She was the last princess to wear the 'kirtle' – a long strip of ermine edged with velvet and worn down the front of the dress. It matched the ermine and velvet of her train. She wore this once more, in 1911, at the Coronation of her nephew King George V.

Grand Duchess Vladimir of Russia, in court dress, St. Petersburg, 1896. As a girl, Princess Marina loved to play with her grandmother's jewels, getting enormous pleasure from the large sparkling diamonds, emeralds and other precious stones. The Grand Duchess's large cache of jewels had been left behind in Russia following the Revoluation when she fled to Switzerland. They were later spirited out of the Vladimir Palace, St. Petersburg, by Bertie Stopford, a young English friend of the Grand Duchess. Queen Mary bought some of the jewels, including a tiara of diamonds with pearl drops, which is often worn by the Queen today.

Dressed to attend a 'Court', Princess Arthur of Connaught looks uncharacteristically glamorous. More at home in stalking tweeds or a nurse's uniform complete with kidney basin, the Princess only put on 'all the trappings' when it was unavoidable. She is wearing a tiara which had been a present from the King and Queen at her marriage in 1913. The jewelled belt and buckle are very much of the 1920s period.

Princess Maud of Fife taken about the time of her marriage to Lord Carnegie, 1923. At this time, only married ladies would wear a tiara; in consequence, Princess Maud has a much simpler bandeau around her head. Even more so than her sister Princess Arthur, she was much happier in sensible country clothes; avoiding the cigarette-smoking, cocktail drinking, fast set of her generation.

Princess Alice Countess of Athlone wearing a tiara over a silk turban. Always one for having fun, the Princess demonstrates an unusual marriage of jewels and fabric. It is probable that the tiara was borrowed for the occasion. None of her descendants who remember her well, have ever seen it, nor have any other photographs of this particular jewel come to light so far.

A Night at the Opera. The Duchess of Gloucester, the Earl of Athlone, the Duke of Gloucester and Princess Alice Countess of Athlone, late 1930s. The men are wearing the Sash and Star of the Most Noble Order of the Garter, while the ladies are wearing the Sash and Star of the Order of the British Empire, which both were awarded in the 1937 Coronation Honours list.

In readiness for the Coronation of King George VI and Queen Elizabeth, 1937, a group taken at Clarence House. Left to right: Alexander Ramsay, who was a page to his cousin, the King, Lady Patricia Ramsay, Crown Princess Ingrid of Denmark wearing the family order of her father-in-law, King Christian X, and Crown Prince Frederick of Denmark who is wearing the chain of Denmark's highest order of chivalry – the Order of the Elephant. He also wears the Sash and Star of the Royal Victorian Order. Although Lady Patricia had divested herself of her royal styles and titles upon her marriage, she attended two subsequent Coronations attired as a Princess of the Blood Royal, riding in the carriage procession of the princes and princesses and walking in their procession within Westminster Abbey.

Princess Marie Louise at the Coronation of King George VI. Her magnificent velvet train was edged by a thick band of fur. She and her sister, Helena Victoria, also walked in the procession of Princes and Princesses of the Blood Royal, though, in reality, they held no territorial designation and were not even Princesses of Great Britain. They were the last members of the royal family to use the style of 'Highness'.

Lady Pamela Mountbatten as Lady-in-Waiting assists the Queen at Melbourne Town Hall, 1954. Lady Pamela, who accompanied the Queen on her long Commonwealth Tour of 1953–54, had also been with her in Kenya in 1952 when Elizabeth heard of the death of her father. The Queen wears the tiara Queen Mary had bought from the estate of Grand Duchess Vladimir of Russia. On this occasion, the pearl drops have been substituted with the Cambridge emeralds.

The Coronation of Queen Elizabeth II, 2nd June 1953: Probably, the largest royal gathering ever photographed in the Throne Room of Buckingham Palace, left to right: the Duchess of Beaufort, the Hereditary Grand Duchess and Hereditary Grand Duke of Luxembourg, the Prince of Liege, Princess Marie Louise, Princess Alice Countess of Athlone, the Duke of Beaufort, Colonel Sir Henry Abel Smith, Princess Alexandra and Prince Michael of Kent, the Duke of Kent, the Duchess of Kent, Lady May Abel Smith, Prince Axel of Denmark, Crown Princess Martha and Crown Prince Olav of Norway, Princess Axel of Denmark, Princess Margaret, Princess Astrid of Norway, Princess Beatrix of Hohenlohe-Langenburg (partly obscured), Prince Kraft of Hohenlohe-Langenburg, Princess Margarita of Baden, The Queen, the Duke of Edinburgh, Princess Margarita of Hohenlohe-Langenburg (whose tiara hides Prince Georg of Hanover), Prince Bernhard of the Netherlands, Princess Sophie of Hanover, Queen Elizabeth the Queen Mother, Lady Helena Gibbs, the Margrave of Baden, Princess Christina of Hesse, the Earl of Athlone (partly obscuring Prince Max of Baden), the Duke of Gloucester, the Princess Royal, the Duchess of Gloucester, the Earl of Harewood, Prince Bertil of Sweden, the Hon.Gerald Lascelles, the Countess of Harewood, Lady Patricia Ramsay, Captain Alexander Ramsay, Admiral the Hon. Sir Alexander Ramsay, Countess and Earl Mountbatten of Burma almost hiding Lady Mary and Mr. Peter Whitley, Lord Brabourne, Lady Pamela Mountbatten, Lady Brabourne and Princess Marie and Prince George of Greece. In front: Prince Charles, Princess Anne and Princes Richard and William of Gloucester. At the very last moment, the Mountbattens swept in, standing in front of the Whitleys almost hiding them completely. 'I'm surprised that Dickie and Edwina haven't brought their dogs to be photographed', Lady Mary Whitley retorted.

INDEX

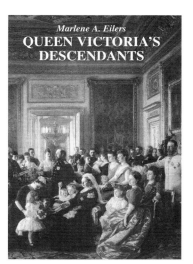
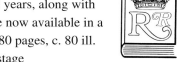